Simplifying Child Development

+

Adolescent Brain 101

2-in-1

A Stage-by-Stage Guide to Nurturing a
Healthy Child's Mind from Embryo to Teen
for Parents and Educators

Joyce T.

may not be suitable for your situation. You should consult with a professional when appropriate. Neither the publisher nor the author shall be liable for any loss of profit or any other commercial damages, including but not limited to special, incidental, consequential, personal, or other damages.

SIMPLIFYING CHILD DEVELOPMENT

ADOLESCENT BRAIN
101

SIMPLIFYING

CHILD

DEVELOPMENT

A Stage-by-Stage Guide to Nurturing a Healthy Child's Mind from Embryo to Teen

Joyce T.

INTRODUCTION

So, you're either gearing up for the wild ride of parenthood or knee-deep in the confusing mess of raising a kiddo – no worries, we're in this together!

Parenting is like trying to assemble IKEA furniture without the manual: challenging, a bit frustrating, but ultimately rewarding. From the moment that little stick gives you the thumbs up, your brain goes into overdrive. How do I not mess this up? What's the secret sauce to raising a happy and healthy kid? How do I navigate this crazy world of child development?

Let me share a story that might sound like yours:

A while back, I was standing in a bookstore, surrounded by a zillion parenting books. It was like trying to choose a flavor at an ice cream shop: overwhelming and a little anxiety-inducing. I realized that parenting might be a bit more complicated than I initially thought. No one-size-fits-all manual could handle the rollercoaster of raising a tiny human.

Fast forward through the sleepless nights and diaper changes; I found out that parenting is a bit like learning to ride a bike. Sure, you might fall a few times, but you get the hang of it. This book is me handing you a shiny new helmet and a roadmap for the journey. Not just any roadmap! This map is for rookies like us.

Deciding to become a parent or already in the whirlwind of diapers and baby giggles? Welcome to a journey that's like no other. From the emotional whirlwind of deciding to become a parent to the awe-inspiring journey of embryo development, we're breaking it down without the confusing jargon. *Simplifying Child Development* is a survival guide for the adorable chaos, with tips on managing first words, early play, and handling the toddler drama.

As your kiddo grows, we tackle the preteen puzzle, decoding hormonal rollercoasters and navigating the maze of friendships. Then, it's onto building a resilient brain, handling everything from homework stress to tricky social situations.

And for the grand finale: teenage hood. Your kid is transforming into a full-blown teenager, seeking independence like a superhero reaching for their cape. We're here to guide you through the delicate dance of giving them wings while keeping them close. You and your teen will form unbreakable bonds before they prepare for the world.

This is your cheat sheet for navigating the ups and downs of child development. Grab your metaphorical parenting cape; we've got a journey to tackle to simplify the adventure of parenthood. As we jump into this adventure, remember that parenting is an ever-changing process and every kid is a unique puzzle. This guide is your cheat sheet, your secret weapon to navigate the ups and downs of child development and raise a happy kiddo. Grab your parenting cape — we have a journey to tackle!

The Marvel of Child Development: A Glance at Your Journey Ahead

Child development unfolds like a captivating story, a tale of a tiny seed transforming into a sapling and blossoming into a towering tree, each stage unraveling unique magic and mystery. From the first heartbeat in the womb to the tumultuous teenage years marked by self-discovery, the journey is a tapestry of precious moments. Much like a complex puzzle lacking a picture on the box, it can leave us feeling both in awe and a bit perplexed.

Imagine witnessing the very first heartbeat echoing in the sanctuary of the womb, a delicate rhythm marking the beginning of an extraordinary adventure. This initial stage, where life quietly takes form, sets the foundation for the entire narrative. From those earliest days, the journey progresses, akin to turning the pages of an enthralling book. As your little one transitions from the protected cocoon of the womb to the outside world, the magic continues to unfold. The toddler years bring forth a cacophony of first words, giggles, and adorable first steps. It is a stage where curiosity dances in their eyes, every discovery like unearthing hidden treasures.

The early childhood phase is the equivalent of the sapling spreading its branches. In this chapter of the developmental narrative, imagination runs wild, friendships are forged, and the world becomes a canvas for creativity. The child, much like the flourishing sapling, explores the environment by absorbing nutrients to fuel the blossoming personality.

The preteen years usher in a stage akin to the tree strengthening its roots. It's a period marked by hormonal changes, self-discovery, and the formation of identity. This phase, much like the intricate network of roots securing the tree, lays the groundwork for the individual your child is destined to become. The teenage years, the grand crescendo of this developmental symphony, are marked by the pursuit of independence. Like the tree standing tall against the wind, your teenager strives to carve their path, navigating the complexities of adolescence. It is a time of blossoming independence and the gradual unfurling of wings.

 For all its marvels, the journey of child development can sometimes lack direction, leading to questions that desire a clear understanding of the challenges at hand. This is a companion through the enchanting and bewildering journey of parenting.

As we delve into child development, let's embrace each stage and navigate the complexities with curiosity, patience, and a profound appreciation for the extraordinary journey of parenthood.

Why This Book: Understanding its Unique Approach

I've walked the path you're on now; navigating the highs of joy, the pangs of anxiety, and the constant hum of uncertainty that comes with raising a child. Countless nights were spent in the pursuit of unraveling the enigma of child development. Through years of learning, firsthand experiences, and collaborative ventures with fellow parents and professionals, I've distilled a wealth of knowledge into the pages of this book.

Consider this book a heart-to-heart conversation between us. It is a space where stories are shared, questions are asked, and answers are found. My aim is to take intricate theories and transform them into bite-sized, easily digestible nuggets of wisdom. This book is crafted to make your journey through the intricate world of child development manageable and enjoyable.

Getting the Most Out of This Book

This book is made simple for you by following the natural order of child development; from a tiny embryo to those tricky teenage years. Remember, every kid is different and doesn't always follow a strict schedule.

You may be asking, "What is your mission?" I want to make this whole parenting thing a breeze for you. No matter how tricky it gets, always remember you are growing along with them and discovering things about yourself that you may have never known!

Are you ready to embark on this adventure of child development? Let us make this journey a fun ride — buckle up!

THE WOMB: THE FIRST HOME

Have you ever wondered why brothers or sisters from the same household end up totally different? Or why one kid might have more allergies than their pals? Before we start breathing, a bunch of stuff is going on that shapes who we turn out to be. Welcome to the awesome world of how babies grow in the womb!

1.1 The Basics of Baby Building

Right from the start, when a tiny cell splits into two, then four, then eight, a whole little person starts forming. This cool process is called prenatal development and it takes about nine months, divided into two parts: the embryonic stage and the fetal stage.

Embryonic Stage

The embryonic stage kicks off from the second week after the magical moment of fertilization until the end of the eighth week. During this short time, a single cell turns into an embryo with a mini brain, spinal cord, and heart. It is like drawing up blueprints and laying down the foundation for a house. Anything wonky happening during this period can cause big problems, as a shaky foundation can mess up a house.

Fetal Stage

The fetal stage occurs from the ninth week until the day of birth. During this period, the house begins to be built. All of the organs and systems from the embryonic stage start growing up. By the end of the 12th week, the fetus appears as a fully formed human, but much smaller. As the weeks continue, the baby keeps growing and preparing for life outside the mom's belly.

Genetics – Our Blueprint

Genes, the stuff we inherit from mom and dad, play a big role in this baby-making process. Genes decide traits such as hair color, eye color, and how tall we might end up. They also have a say in what diseases we could be prone to, our mood, and what we enjoy.

Think of genes as the building materials for the house. If these materials are not up to code, the baby or the home may encounter problems down the road.

Environment – The Paint and Neighborhood

The surroundings, both inside and outside the mom, are crucial to the baby's development. The inside environment is how healthy and happy the mom is. Things such as food intake, stress levels, and being around harmful chemicals can affect the baby growing inside her. Imagine painting the walls of your new house. The type of paint applied can change the safety of the home. The food, drinks, and medicine the mom ingests are the paint for the growing baby, impacting its health.

The outside environment is like the neighborhood where the house is built. If the outside environment is safe and pleasant, the home life improves, helping the baby thrive during development.

Prenatal development shows off the amazing power of nature and life. As we uncover the secrets of this process, we better understand how complicated and awesome human development is.

1.2 Keeping Mom Healthy: A Parent's Guide to Growing Babies

The Magic of Good Nutrition

Think of the nutrients a mom eats as the building blocks for her growing baby. Trying to build a baby without the right nutrients is like building a house without bricks — a total no-go! Good nutrition is incredibly important for ensuring the baby's structures form correctly. Protein helps the cells grow and form as the foundation for the baby's physical development. Iron helps form the placenta and moves oxygen to the baby. Folic acid lowers the risk of some problems. But here's the catch: too much of something such as Vitamin A can create problems — balance is crucial.

The Stress Story: When Alarms Don't Stop Ringing

Stress is a part of life; when it's too much during pregnancy, it's like having a never-ending alarm in the house — exhausting! Think about living in a home where the alarm never stops. The constant stress from the noise puts the body on high alert and can affect how the baby grows. Chronic stress can mess with certain hormones that might affect the baby's developing brain. Stress can also lead to low birth weight and preterm birth. Some occasional stress is normal and not a problem; it is the constant, never-ending stress that can create issues.

Mom's Choices Matter: The Lifestyle Edition

A mom's lifestyle choices truly matter for her baby's growth. Smoking is like building a dream house in a polluted city — not great! The harmful chemicals from smoke can harm the baby's growth and cause issues such as low birth weight and preterm birth. Alcohol is another substance that can lead to developmental issues.. Drinking can potentially lead to fetal alcohol spectrum disorders (FASD). FASD includes physical, behavioral, and learning disorders.

Blueprint Inspection Time: Health Check-Ups

Just like checking a new house is safe and sound, moms need regular health check-ups during pregnancy. Routine visits help a mom keep tabs on how the pregnancy is going and how the baby is developing. These visits can catch potential problems early on.

Tests such as ultrasounds spill the beans on the baby's growth and any early signs of issues. Blood tests keep an eye on the mom's health, checking for things including gestational diabetes or preeclampsia that can affect the pregnancy.

Mom's Health: The Superpower for Baby's Future

Mom's health is the secret sauce in making sure the baby grows healthy and happy. As parents, we know diet, stress management, and regular check-ups set the stage for a positive birthing process. . Keep it up parents — you are doing a great job!

1.3 Embracing the Journey: Tips for Expectant Moms

As you embark on this incredible journey of motherhood, here are some nurturing tips for both you and your growing baby:

Balanced Diet: A Rainbow on Your Plate

Picture your plate as a canvas filled with the colors of various fruits and veggies. These foods create a rainbow of vitamins and minerals. Whole grains such as brown rice and oats offer energy-packed carbs. For those crucial building blocks, turn to protein sources including lean meat, fish, eggs, and beans. Do not' forget dairy or calcium-rich alternatives to support your baby's bone and teeth development!

Healthy fats from avocados and nuts are vital for brain development. And of course, stay hydrated with plenty of water! While you can indulge in pregnancy cravings, aim for balance!

Regular Exercise: Navigating the Tightrope

Exercising during pregnancy can be a balancing act. Are you feeling tired? Listen to your body and rest while exercising when you have energy. Exercise can boost your mood, improve sleep, and enhance stamina during labor.

Include low-impact activities such as walking throughout your pregnancy. Prenatal yoga and Pilates classes can enhance flexibility and muscle tone. Swimming provides a weightless experience, taking the load off your growing belly. Mix cardio, strength training, and flexibility exercises; always check with your healthcare provider before starting or continuing any exercise routine.

Adequate Rest: A Must for You and Your Baby

Rest is non-negotiable! Rest helps you recover from the physical changes of pregnancy and provides a peaceful environment for your baby to thrive. Prioritize sleep and aim for 7-9 hours each night. If fatigue hits during the day, listen to your body; indulge in short, rejuvenating naps.

Emotional Well-Being: Nurturing the Heart

Your emotional well-being is vital for creating a positive space for your baby. It is okay for emotions to run high! Find positive activities to release stress: meditate, read, spend time in nature, or chat with a loved one.

Cultivate positive emotions by envisioning moments with your baby. Picture their smiles and anticipate the joy of their presence. This imagery creates a positive emotional atmosphere, surrounding your baby in a cocoon of love and warmth.

Pregnancy: A Journey of Growth for You and Your Baby

Remember, pregnancy is not just about your baby's growth; it is about your growth as a parent. Pregnancy is a transformative time to nurture yourself while nurturing the new life within you. Take care of your physical health, foster emotional balance, and most importantly, savor this unique time. Your baby can feel the ripples of this love even before they're born.

1.4 Unveiling Pregnancy Realities: A Mom's Guide

As we navigate the rollercoaster of pregnancy, let's debunk some common concerns and myths, and I'll sprinkle in a bit of my own experiences — shall we?

Morning Sickness: Beyond Mornings and Myths

Contrary to the name, morning sickness doesn't play by the clock or limit itself to the first trimester. For me, it was more like an all-day queasiness that hung around until well into the second trimester. I found solace in snacking on crackers, opting for smaller meals, and sipping ginger tea. Remember, morning sickness is usually harmless; if you find yourself unable to keep anything down like I did, have a chat with your healthcare provider.

Food Cravings: The Strange, the Sweet, and the Spicy

Craving pickles dipped in chocolate? Well, I was all about the spicy stuff — jalapeños on everything! While some cravings may be your body's way of shouting "I need this!" others, like my occasional craving for ice cream topped with hot sauce, are just plain quirky. It is cool to indulge, as long as it's within reason — balance is key!

Weight Gain: Busting the "Eating for Two" Myth

The "eating for two" idea was a surprise for me. I learned that I only needed around 340 extra calories per day in the second and third trimesters. Gaining weight was a concern — not too much but not too little. I found a balance through regular walks, healthier food choices, and the occasional treat. Regular check-ups with my healthcare provider kept me on track.

Baby's Movement: Every Kick and Flutter is Unique

Feeling those first kicks and flutters was a highlight for me. It happened around the 20th week, and it felt like a gentle tapping from the inside. As the weeks went by, those taps turned into full-blown somersaults. My baby had a unique rhythm; paying attention to that rhythm was fascinating and reassuring.

Amid the sea of pregnancy advice, remember that every journey is unique. Listen to your body, trust your instincts, and keep chatting with your healthcare provider. You're not just growing a baby; you're growing into your role as a parent. This is a time of discovery, transformation, and anticipation. Take a deep breath, embrace the changes, and get ready for the incredible journey ahead.

BABY STEPS: BIRTH TO ONE YEAR

Imagine standing at the edge of a huge, blank canvas with a bunch of colors in your hand, ready to create something amazing. Just like the canvas, your baby's brain is a blank slate waiting to soak up all sorts of experiences. The first year of their life is a super-fast journey of transformation, crazy growth, and learning new things. In this chapter, we're going to break down the cool milestones your baby will hit during their first year.

2.1 Understanding Infant Milestones: The Masterpiece Unfolds

Motor Skills: From Tummy Time to First Steps

In those initial months, your baby gains control over their movements: lifting their head, kicking their legs, and grasping objects. Around six months, rolling over, sitting with support, and reaching for objects become the norm. Towards the end of the first year, crawling, standing, and the first steps may grace the scene.

Sensory Development: A Symphony of Senses

From birth, your baby experiences the world through sight, hearing, touch, taste, and smell. Picture their vision as a fogged-up window, gradually clearing over the year. They focus on objects 8-12 inches away; this is the perfect distance to your face during feeds. Their hearing sharpens, turning towards sounds and responding to their name. Touch becomes a language of love, shaping bonds through skin-to-skin contact and gentle massages.

Cognitive Growth: The Brain's Artistic Journey

Your baby's brain is a sponge, soaking up information. In the early months, they recognize faces and respond to expressions. By six months, cause-and-effect relationships come into play: shaking a rattle makes a sound, dropping a toy makes it disappear. Towards the end of the year, imitation of sounds, waving bye-bye, and understanding simple instructions unfold, marking the beginning of cognitive development.

Social Interactions: The Heartwarming Symphony

The social journey begins with that first smile, usually between 6-12 weeks, warming hearts and strengthening bonds. As your baby grows, they respond to emotions, giggle, and play peek-a-boo. By the end of the first year, signs of anxiety around strangers and clinginess to familiar faces emerge.

The first year is a masterpiece in the making; a period of rapid transformation and growth. Understanding these milestones allows you to be the curator, providing the support your baby needs at each stage and celebrating their unique progress.

2.2 Nourishing Your Little One: From Breast Milk to Solid Adventures

Feeding your baby is a fascinating journey from breastfeeding to the world of solids. Let's explore the key points to ensure your baby gets the best start in their nourishment.

Benefits of Breastfeeding: Building a Strong Foundation

Breast milk is a powerhouse of nutrients and antibodies that work wonders for your baby's immune system, providing protection against various common illnesses.

Introduction to Solids: Opening a Gastronomic World

Around the six-month mark as your baby's nutritional needs grow, you will need to introduce solid foods. This marks the beginning of a culinary adventure, exposing your little one to a variety of tastes and textures. Starting with purees and progressing to mashed and finger foods, the introduction of solids should be a gradual and patient process. The process is not only nutrition; you are teaching your baby the art of eating, helping them understand hunger and fullness cues. During this transition, you are laying the foundation for healthy eating habits.

Allergies and Food Sensitivities: Safely Navigating New Flavors

As you venture into the world of different foods, keeping an eye on potential allergies and sensitivities is crucial. Common allergenic foods such as cow's milk, eggs, peanuts, tree nuts, soy, wheat, fish, and shellfish should be introduced one at a time, with a few days in between to monitor reactions. Watch out for signs like hives, vomiting, diarrhea, or swelling around the mouth. Severe reactions may include difficulty breathing or loss of consciousness, which requires immediate medical attention. Food sensitivities may manifest as a rash, fussiness, or mild digestive issues. Remember, allergies can develop at any time; stay observant, even if a particular food has been well-tolerated before.

Hydration Needs: Quenching Thirst Naturally

For the first six months, breast milk or formula covers all your baby's hydration needs, providing a perfectly balanced thirst-quencher. When you introduce solids, offering small amounts of water gradually becomes part of the routine. While fruit juice may seem like a healthy option, it's high in sugar and can fill up your baby, leaving less room for nutritious foods. Think of it as choosing between a healthy smoothie and a soda. This period is all about fostering a positive relationship between your baby and a nutritious diet.

2.3 Nurturing a Strong Connection: Insights from a Mother's Journey

Just as a seed needs the right soil to grow, an infant requires a nurturing environment to form a strong emotional bond. This bond is known as *attachment.* Attachment acts as a secure base from which your baby can explore the world. Drawing from personal experiences as a mother, let's delve into the practical aspects of cultivating secure attachment.

Responsive Caregiving: The Dance of Connection

Attuning to your baby's needs and responding promptly and appropriately is akin to a dance where your baby leads and you follow. This dance of responsiveness sends a powerful message: "You are important. Your needs matter. You can trust me." Whether your baby cries out of hunger, fusses due to a wet diaper, or simply needs a cuddle, each response from you helps them feel secure and loved.

I vividly remember those late-night cries. Responding promptly not only soothed my baby but also strengthened our bond.

Consistent Routine: Stability Amidst the Roller Coaster

Life with a newborn is like a roller coaster with ups, downs, and unexpected twists. Amid this unpredictability, establishing a consistent routine can provide a sense of security and predictability for your baby. Our bedtime routine, including a warm bath and a lullaby, became a cherished time for connection and signaled that it was time to wind down.

Physical Affection: The Language of Love

Physical affection, from skin-to-skin contact to daily cuddles, is the universal language of love that every baby understands. As your baby grows, this affection evolves, contributing to a strong emotional connection and improved overall well-being.

Those tender moments of cuddling and playful tickles not only brought joy but also strengthened our emotional bond.

Emotional Availability: Understanding and Responding

Being emotionally available for your baby involves being present, attentive, and empathetic to their feelings. Observing their cues, practicing empathy, and responding in a loving and supportive manner form the foundation for emotional development. Learning to decipher my baby's unique language of smiles, cries, and coos helped me respond more effectively to their needs.

Cultivating secure attachment is an ongoing journey, marked by moments of connection and understanding. Your baby's emotional development is nurtured through these experiences, fostering confidence and resilience for their journey ahead. Similarly, these insights from personal experiences as a mother shed light on the practical aspects of building a strong and secure attachment with your little one.

2.4 Navigating Common Challenges in the Journey of Parenthood

Parenting a newborn can feel like solving a complex puzzle, the pieces changing every day. These challenges can leave you feeling puzzled and overwhelmed. Let's explore common infant issues and strategies to navigate these intricate terrains, with a closer look at real-life examples.

Sleep Issues: Crafting a Restful Routine

Newborns sleep in short bursts, waking frequently to feed regardless of the time, creating uneven sleep for parents. Around 3-6 months, babies often start consolidating their sleep, aligning with night and day. I successfully established a bedtime routine with a warm bath and a lullaby.

Colic and Reflux: Weathering the Storm

Colic, like a mysterious storm, can bring prolonged crying, while reflux causes discomfort and spit-ups. Both challenges usually resolve in 3-4 months. When my baby had colic, I held them and adjusted feeding positions to ease reflux symptoms.

Teething: A Milestone in Discomfort

Teething, a major milestone, can cause discomfort with symptoms including drooling and irritability. I provided a chilled teething ring for my baby during this period, similar to a cold pack for a sore muscle.

Separation Anxiety: Supporting Emotional Growth

Around the second half of the first year, babies often experience separation anxiety, exhibiting clinginess or crying when separated. Strategies for coping include:

Practicing brief separations helped my baby adjust to the idea that I could go away and return, fostering emotional growth.

Navigating these challenges is an ongoing journey, and every baby is unique. The key is to adapt and discover what works best for your little one. Parenthood is a dynamic puzzle, with each piece contributing to the beautiful picture of your baby's growth and development.

As we conclude this chapter on "Baby Steps — Birth to One Year," we're reminded that every little journey begins with a single step; the first year of your baby's life is a remarkable expedition filled with growth, discovery, and boundless love. From the first cries to the first steps, each milestone is a testament to the incredible journey you and your baby have embarked upon together. As a parent, relish these precious moments, savor the triumphs, and navigate the challenges with the confidence that you're laying a strong foundation for a lifetime of adventures ahead. Embrace the joy, cherish the memories, and get ready for the next chapter of your extraordinary parenting odyssey. Here's to celebrating the magic of baby steps!

INTO TODDLERHOOD: ONE TO THREE YEARS

Have you ever seen a baby bird take its first flight? It is waiting for something exciting, feeling all jittery, and then being totally amazed when it finally spreads its wings. Now, imagine that same kind of anticipation and excitement when your little one starts toddling around. They're not babies anymore; they are tiny adventurers ready to explore a whole new world.

As a mother and a writer, this transformation is a beautiful story. Each step they take is a sentence, each discovery a paragraph, and the overall journey a captivating story. You are chronicling the unfolding chapters of your child's unique tale.

3.1 Toddlerhood Unveiled: Navigating the Realm of Exploration

Have you ever marveled at the first flight of a young bird? There's a palpable sense of anticipation, a flutter of excitement, and a breath of awe as it spreads its wings for the first time. This enchanting experience is akin to witnessing your child's transition into toddlerhood. No longer are they merely babies; they are little individuals poised to take flight into a world brimming with curiosities.

Motor Skill Mastery: The Terrain of Exploration

By their first birthday, most toddlers have conquered the art of independent walking. Over the next couple years, their motor skills undergo a remarkable evolution. Picture them running, climbing, and jumping — little explorers conquering the terrain of their world. Moreover, they embark on refining their fine motor skills, expertly holding a spoon, creating crayon masterpieces, and skillfully stacking blocks.

At fifteen months, my toddler began his climbing adventures on the playground, conquering small steps and platforms, filling our days with anxiety and pride.

Cognitive Flourishing: A Tree of Knowledge

As your toddler delves into their surroundings, their cognitive growth unfolds like a tree branching out in all directions. They begin to unravel the mysteries of how things work, exhibit problem-solving skills, and immerse themselves in imaginative play. Picture them experimenting with various block arrangements, turning a simple box into a car or boat during pretend play.

Intrigued by puzzles, my little one discovered how shapes fit together and took joy in transforming a cardboard box into a spaceship.

Language Symphony: The Songbird on Branches

If cognitive growth is the tree, language is the melodious songbird perched on its branches. Toddlerhood contains the captivating transition from babbling to meaningful speech. By their second year, most toddlers begin using words and simple sentences, expressing desires like asking for "milk" or signaling someone's departure with "daddy go." At two, my toddler's vocabulary bloomed, turning our home into a constant chatter of "more," "mine," and "play."

Social Ballet: The Toddler's Dance

Entering the social arena, toddlers grasp the basic rules of the game. They observe, imitate, and gradually learn to interact with others. In early interactions, gestures may include offering a toy or pulling a parent's hand to share a discovery. Recently, my toddler comforted a crying playmate, showcasing an emerging sense of empathy and kindness.

As your baby approaches their third birthday, their social interactions become more intricate, involving parallel play alongside peers and moments of shared joy, empathy, and camaraderie. Witnessing this journey is not just observing growth; it is participating in the magical unfolding of your toddler's unique personality.

3.2 Nurturing Speech and Language Development: Unlocking the World of Words

Vocabulary Expansion: Unveiling the Magic of Words

Around the age of one, toddlers embark on a linguistic adventure, uttering their first meaningful words including "mama," "dada," or "no." However, this is just the beginning of a remarkable journey. Over the next couple of years, their vocabulary magically expands. They progress from naming familiar objects to using action words, describing words, and simple prepositions.

Imagine your toddler pointing at the family pet and excitedly saying "doggy" for the first time. As weeks go by, they may surprise you by adding "big doggy" or "doggy run" to their vocabulary. Create a language-rich environment to foster vocabulary expansion. Read colorful storybooks, sing engaging songs, play rhyming games, and involve them in everyday conversations about their surroundings.

Sentence Formation: Stringing Words Like Pearls

With an expanding vocabulary, toddlers begin stringing words together, forming two-word phrases such as "want milk" or "mommy come." They will gradually progress to longer phrases and sentences, expressing more complex ideas.

Your toddler may start by saying "more cookie" and later articulate the phrase to, "I want more chocolate chip cookies, please." Modeling correct sentence structure during conversations will help the child progress with their vocabulary. If your toddler says "ball gone," expand it into a full sentence: "Yes, the ball has rolled under the couch."

Pronunciation Improvement: From Babble to Clarity

In the early stages, toddlers may simplify words such as saying "nana" for banana. However, as their speech muscles develop, their pronunciation improves. By the age of three, their speech is generally understandable even to those outside the family. Your child may initially say "tat" for cat. After some training, your toddler might progress to saying "I see a cat" more clearly. To help with pronunciation, repeat words correctly when responding to your toddler. For instance, if they say "I see a tat," you could respond, "Yes, you see a cat."

Non-Verbal Communication: Adding Color to Words

Non-verbal communication will add color and context to their words. Toddlers begin using gestures, facial expressions, body language, and tone of voice to convey desires.

Your toddler may point excitedly at a favorite toy, expressing joy without uttering a word. To foster non-verbal communication, respond to gestures, mimic expressions, and use a variety of gestures in your interactions. Pay attention to the tone of your voice, conveying emotions even if the words are not fully understood.

In this journey of speech and language development, your patience, engagement, and celebration of small victories play a pivotal role. As a parent, you're not just teaching your child to communicate; you are nurturing their confidence to express themselves, fostering a unique and beautiful connection.

3.3 Mastering the Potty: A Beginner's Guide for New Parents

Getting Ready

Remember when you first tried riding a bike? Potty training is a bit like that; your little one should take the plunge only when they're good and ready. Look for signs including your toddler getting curious about bathroom stuff or noticing when their diaper is dirty. A regular poop routine is also a clue. It is crucial they can pull their pants up and down and stay dry for at least two hours.

Choosing the Gear

There are a couple of available options. Some parents go for a standalone potty chair: it is low, easy for your tot to use, and just their size. Or you can get a potty seat that fits on your regular toilet. Just make sure it's secure; maybe consider a step stool for their little feet. The choice is up to what your kiddo likes and what's convenient for you.

Getting Into the Swing

Now that you've got the gear, it's time to set up a potty routine. Pick specific times for potty breaks, such as after meals or before bedtime. Encourage your kiddo to sit for a few minutes. If they're not into it, maybe read a book or sing a song to make it fun — no pressure!

Oopsies Happen

Like learning anything new, there will be mess-ups. Accidents will happen, and sometimes they may even backtrack a bit. Stay cool and reassure them when oopsies occur. If they start acting like they've never heard of a potty before, just be patient and keep cheering them on.

Potty Training Victory Lap

Potty training is a big deal for your little one — – a step towards independence. Be patient, celebrate the wins, don't sweat the whoopsies, and enjoy the ride!

3.4 Navigating Toddler Tantrums and Emotions: A Survival Guide for Parents

Unraveling the Mystery

Tantrums are emotional outbursts from your toddler, signaling their frustration or struggles to cope with overwhelming feelings. Maybe they're tired, hungry, or just struggling to communicate effectively.

Imagine your toddler gets upset because they can't have a cookie before dinner. It may not be just about the cookie; they could be hungry or testing boundaries.

Calm Amidst the Storm

When tantrum waves hit, it's a challenge for both you and your toddler. Your presence becomes an anchor, offering comfort and stability.

If your toddler is having a meltdown at the store because you said no to buying a new toy, make sure to stay calm. Reassure them you understand their feelings can make a difference.

Taming the Tantrum Beast

To calm the storm, try these strategies:

— Distraction: Redirect their attention to something positive.

— Deep Breathing: Take deep breaths together to ease tension.

— Quiet Time: Sometimes, they just need a moment to settle down.

— Comforting Gestures: A hug or soothing words can work wonders.

If your toddler is upset because they can't play with a friend, offer to read their favorite book to them. This action may shift their focus and ease disappointment.

Unlocking Emotional Expression

Encourage healthy emotional expression with these approaches:

— Naming Emotions: Help them identify and name what they're feeling.

— Validating Emotions: Acknowledge and show understanding of their feelings.

— Modeling Expression: Demonstrate how to express your emotions appropriately.

If your toddler is sad about saying goodbye to a favorite stuffed animal, have them name their emotion and show empathy for their discomfort.

Fortifying Against Future Tantrums

While you can't dodge every tantrum, understanding triggers can help:

— Stick to a Routine: Manage hunger or tiredness tantrums by maintaining a consistent routine.

— Offer Simple Choices: Provide empowerment by letting them make simple decisions.

— Language-Rich Environment: Encourage expression by fostering a language-rich environment.

Establish a consistent nap routine for your toddler in order to prevent them from throwing a tantrum.

Every child is unique — trial and error is a must! Embrace the tantrum journey with patience; soon you'll become a pro at riding the emotional waves of toddlerhood!

As we come to the close of this chapter, I invite you to pause and contemplate the incredible metamorphosis your child is experiencing in these toddler years. From those tentative first steps to the emergence of coherent sentences, from the triumph of successful potty training to the rollercoaster ride of their first full-blown tantrum, each moment unfolds as a testament to your child's blossoming abilities and your steadfast support. This journey is nothing short of a magical adventure, adorned with a tapestry of firsts, sprinkled with challenges, and saturated with an abundance of love, laughter, and learning. Embrace this rollercoaster, relish the fleeting moments, and eagerly anticipate the captivating chapters awaiting your child's development.

THE PRESCHOOL PHASE: THREE TO FIVE YEARS

In this chapter, we are going to dive into the preschool phase — buckle up! We are going to chat about how your child's brainpower amps up, why playing pretend is their secret weapon for learning stuff, how hanging out with other little humans shapes their social game, and how they start understanding the rollercoaster of feelings. We are on a mission to get you in the know about your kid's growth, so you're all set to have their back and enjoy every bit of the journey. Are you ready — let's roll!

4.1 Navigating the Preschool Mind and Playground

Problem-Solving Prowess

Think of your kid's problem-solving skills like a superhero's compass on their adventurous journey. In preschool, these skills go through the roof. Picture this: they're figuring out how to build a tower of blocks that doesn't crash down. Or maybe they're plotting a genius move to grab a toy sitting on the tippy-top shelf, possibly involving a stool and some climbing action.

During this learning period, their block tower may keep collapsing, causing them to try different methods for stability. They may spot a toy out of reach and get creative by grabbing a stool and grabbing the object. The child's problem-solving ability grows through experimentation.

The Theater of Imagination

Imagine your living room transforming into a zoo, library, or a spaceship soaring through galaxies — that is the magic of imagination! During the preschool phase, your kid becomes a master of make-believe. They might play doctor, giving check-ups to their stuffed buddies and diagnose them with a case of the "giggles." They could be a master chef, creating the most amazing pretend dishes you have ever had. Your child's imagination will create wonderful scenarios for both of you to enjoy!

— Example 1: They might diagnose their teddy bear with a case of the "giggles" and prescribe lots of laughter.

— Example 2: In their make-believe kitchen, they're the chef concocting the most fantastical pretend dishes you've ever "tasted."

Playground Diplomacy

Just like travelers swapping stories, your kiddo learns a ton by hanging out with their little buddies. These interactions are a crash course in social skills. Whether sharing toys during a playdate, teaming up to build a sandcastle, or comforting a friend who's feeling blue, the playground is their training ground.

For example, kids will learn the art of sharing when one of their buddies wants to take a turn with the superhero action figure. Going further, they decide they want to create the ultimate sandbox fortress to have a home for the action figure. In this scenario, the kids learned cooperation and decision making through one simple action.

Emotion Ocean Navigation

Picture your child as the captain of a tiny boat navigating the vast ocean of emotions. In preschool, they begin learning the ropes, recognizing feelings, and figuring out how to steer through them.

Instead of throwing a tantrum when upset, they calmly say, "I feel sad because I wanted the blue crayon." Or they may seek their favorite stuffed animal if feeling a bit overwhelmed. Your child's cognitive functioning is developing right before your eyes!

4.2 Nurturing Creativity and Imagination: Unleashing the Inner Picasso

Crafty Adventures

Let us discuss arts and crafts, where your preschooler's creativity blooms like a sunflower in full swing. A box of crayons isn't just for coloring; it's a ticket to creating a vibrant rainbow on paper. And what about that lump of clay? It is a sculptor's dream, ready to transform into fascinating creatures. Watch the intense focus as they cut along a line, hear the excitement when they mix paint to make a new color, and witness the pride when they unveil their masterpiece.

Make-Believe Narratives

In the realm of pretend play, a regular afternoon becomes a full-blown adventure. A tea party with teddy bears, a daring rescue mission led by superhero action figures, or a journey to the moon in a cardboard spaceship; the possibilities are as vast as their imagination. They are not just playing; they are storytellers, creating scenarios, developing characters, and narrating a sequence of events. They can create a tea party where stuffed animals are the VIPs or transform the living room into a superhero headquarters with incredible missions and heroic deeds.

Musical Joyride

The notes of music and dance are the universal languages of pure joy. Picture your child as a one-person band, singing their favorite nursery rhyme while shaking a makeshift tambourine, creating a musical fiesta right in the living room. . Through music and dance, they express feelings, enhance motor skills, and just revel in the sheer joy of movement.

— Example 1: Beltin' out their favorite nursery rhyme while giving an impromptu dance performance.

— Example 2: Shaking a makeshift tambourine during a family dance party in the living room, creating a mini musical fiesta.

Outdoor Adventures

The great outdoors is a boundless playground for your little explorer. Nature becomes their canvas for connecting, sensing, and letting curiosity run wild. They may spot a caterpillar, sparking an impromptu storytelling session, or use sticks and stones to create a masterpiece during a family picnic. Every outdoor escapade opens doors to endless learning and imaginative possibilities.

4.3 Getting Ready for School: The ABCs of Essential Skills

So your child is gearing up for the big school adventure, and there are a few skills they must grasp before diving in. Think of it like they're little detectives, figuring out the secrets of letters and numbers.

Spotting ABCs and 123s

Each letter has its own sound; as your kiddo starts recognizing them, they begin to open the door to the world of reading and writing. Numbers on the other hand, are the language of logic and order. Knowing them sets the stage for thinking all math-like.

Your child becomes a detective when they point at a letter on a cereal box and say, "Look, Mom, it's the letter 'A'!"

Playing with Pencils

Now, your little artist is ready to rock the pencil scene. At first, their writing may look like squiggles — similar to their first steps. With some practice and cool writing tools, they'll be crafting legible letters like a pro. You might find doodles all over your grocery list. When you ask, "What's this?" your kiddo proudly says, "I wrote my name, see!"

Listen Up and Do Stuff

As your child steps into the school world, being a good listener and following instructions is like having a superpower. It is not just about hearing; it's about grasping what's being said and responding properly. Playing games, chatting about stories, and paying attention during talks help develop these skills. When you play a game of "Simon Says" and your kiddo nails all the moves, they are flexing their listening muscles!

Friends and Sharing Vibes

While reading books is valuable, the development of social skills plays the greatest role in your child's development. Like trees need roots, your kiddo needs strong social skills. Sharing toys, taking turns, and being a buddy to others are the social threads weaving the classroom fabric. When your child shares their snack with a friend or helps a buddy tie their shoelaces, that's the social superhero emerging!

So, that's the scoop on getting your little explorer all set for the school scene. ABCs, 123s, pencils, listening ears, and good vibes – they're ready to rock and roll!

4.4 Navigating Preschool Hiccups: Your Go-To Guide

Let us tackle some of the tricky stuff that comes with preschool territory. Little ones can be like volcanoes, bursting with all kinds of emotions. Here's the lowdown on how to handle a few common challenges.

Homesick Blues

So, your kiddo's got the separation sads? This is totally normal! Give them a big hug, flash a confident smile, and reassure them that you'll be back. Make goodbyes quick and reassuring — routine helps! As always, sprinkle on loads of love and affection to keep their sense of security intact. Maybe when you pick them up, you can say, "See? I told you I'd come back, just like we practiced!"

Tiny Tornado Tantrums

Preschoolers are like emotional volcanoes, Preschoolers occasionally turn to hitting, biting, or full-on tantrums to show emotion. Remember, they're not being bad; they're just wrestling with all these big feelings. Set clear boundaries, use timeouts to cool things down, and encourage them to use words instead of unleashing a mini tornado. When they calm down after a timeout and say, "I'm mad because I wanted the blue cup," that's the words-in-action victory!

Scary Shadows and Bedtime Battles

Is your child seeing monsters under the bed or scary shadows in the dark? These visions are part of the imagination rollercoaster. Reassure them, validate those fears, and maybe toss in a comforting toy or nightlight to ease the spooky vibes. If they insist on checking under the bed for monsters, you can join the monster hunt together — turn it into a little adventure!

Bedtime Struggles: The Great Sleep Showdown

Bedtime can be like climbing Mount Everest for preschoolers. They might resist, demand a zillion bedtime stories, or become nighttime escape artists. Want to know the secret weapon for this challenge? A consistent bedtime routine that turns bedtime into a cozy, predictable hill rather than a battleground. Maybe create a little bedtime ritual like reading a favorite book or sharing a silly bedtime joke to make it a fun routine they look forward to!

So, there you have it! Your own e cheat sheet to navigate preschool speed bumps. Hugs, boundaries, and a sprinkle of imagination magic can turn these challenges into conquerable hills!

And here we are fellow moms and dads on this adventure through the preschool years! We have dove into the world of crayon doodles, make-believe tea parties, and tackled the bedtime routine with our little dragons. As we finish up this chapter, let's appreciate the wonderful experience our kids are having. From those first crayon strokes to the nightly negotiations with bedtime creatures, every moment is a valuable step in our children's growth and understanding. We have explored cognitive milestones, nurtured creativity, and gathered strategies for handling the inevitable bumps along the way.

THE ELEMENTARY YEARS: 6 TO 11 YEARS

In this chapter, we'll dig into the noticeable shifts in your child's thinking and emotions during the elementary school years. We will explore the growth of executive functions, the development of skills for handling emotions, how screen time affects brain development, and why play plays a critical role in shaping cognitive abilities.

5.1 Navigating Brain Growth: Changes in Thinking and Feelings

Mastering the Brain's Orchestra: Executive Functions

Think of your child's brain during the elementary years like a musician learning to play a fancy tune. They are not just rocking the ABCs; they're diving into projects, planning their moves, staying focused despite the chaos, and handling frustration like champs. It is like your kid is becoming a brain maestro, learning to plan stuff and stay cool even when things get a bit messy. Building a model airplane or playing a board game can be good brain workouts, helping them get better at this cool brain symphony.

Emotions 101: The Art of Emotional Regulation

Emotional regulation is the ability to control your feelings. Your elementary kiddo is leveling up by recognizing more complicated emotions in themselves and others, figuring out what triggers those feelings, and understanding better ways to respond. They are getting better at knowing when they feel things, understanding why, and finding the right way to deal with it. Make it easy for them by talking about feelings, saying it's okay to feel things, and showing them how it's done.

Screens and Brain Sunlight: The Balance Game

In our world of screens, your kid's brain is a little plant. Just like sunlight helps it grow, the right amount of screen time is cool. But too much? That can be like pouring too much water – not great.

Screens are everywhere; too much exposure is like too many cookies — not good! Excessive screen time can mess with their attention span, creativity, and how they interact with other kids. Make sure they have time limits, watch stuff that's okay for their age, and mix it up with other fun things such as playing outside or building a LEGO tower.

Playtime: The Brain's Favorite Playground

For kids, play is their secret power. It is how they explore, learn cool stuff, and get super smart. As your elementary kiddo grows up, their play gets even cooler; they begin to enjoy make-believe adventures, tricky puzzles, and games with rules.

Play helps your child learn and become super smart. Give them cool toys, play with them, and let them have time to just mess around. It is like brain exercise but much more fun!

5.2 Cultivating the Love for Learning: Academic Wins and Strategies

Unlocking the Magic of Words: Reading and Literacy Skills

From recognizing letters to diving into stories, your kid's journey into reading is a gradual adventure. Reading to them, chatting about tales, and making guesses about what happens next are awesome ways to make this reading magic happen. Reading books together and talking about the stories will help improve their ability to piece information together.

Math Mania: Making Numbers Fun

As your elementary kiddo grows, so too does their math brain. They go from numbers to complete mathematical thinking: adding,adding, subtracting, dealing with fractions, and measuring things. They begin to spot patterns and solve puzzles — like a math superhero! Counting cookies while baking, playing board games, or even sorting socks are strong ways to train their math powers.

Crafty Learning: The Power of Creative Arts

Creative arts aren't just fun; they are a workout for your child's imagination and brain. Get your kiddo to show what they know with creative stuff such as painting scenes from stories or building cool clay models of science things. Creative arts are their secret brain workout; let them draw or make stuff to show what they learned. This will help them turn their ideas into cool art!

Homework Highway: Strategies for Success

Homework is like a bridge connecting school and home; however, crossing it can be a bit complicated. To make the process easier, set up a regular homework routine. Create a quiet spot, gather all the gear, and remind them to take small breaks. You're there for support but let them take the lead. Homework is a bit like walking on a bridge between school and home.

Create a comfy homework spot, take small breaks, and remember that you're there to cheer them on, not do all the work.

With these cool strategies, you're not just helping your kiddo do well in school; you are also setting them up with awesome life skills. They will learn how to manage time, be disciplined, and never give up!

5.3 Navigating Everyday Challenges in the Elementary Years

Tackling Fear and Anxiety

Think of your child's elementary years as an epic journey with towering mountains and deep rivers — opportunities and challenges at every turn. As your little explorer faces new territories, fears and anxieties might pop up like intimidating obstacles. When these alarms go off frequently, it can be distressing. Help your child express their feelings openly and break down fears into manageable parts. Reassure them by providing coping strategies to prepare for the challenge.

Balancing Screen Time

In today's world, screens are as common as trees in a forest. While they offer educational benefits, too much screen time can lead to issues. Your child is getting lost in the digital forest, missing out on other beautiful landscapes.

Maintain a balanced digital diet by setting screen time limits and monitor content. Encourage outdoor play, reading, and family time, guiding your child to explore the entire landscape, not just the digital forest.

Healthy Eating Habits

Just as a tree needs sunlight, water, and nutrients, your child needs a balanced diet. During the elementary years, picky eating or unbalanced diets may emerge, like favoring one nutrient in the soil. Involve your child in meal planning and let them help in the garden, nurturing their interest. Offer a variety of foods, like adding different nutrients to the soil. Model healthy eating habits, creating a positive mealtime environment to show your child how to care for the garden.

Encouraging Physical Activity

Physical activity is the wind beneath your child's wings, boosting their overall well-being. In elementary years, they should be spreading their wings through sports, biking, or play, soaring higher with each gust of wind.

Foster an active lifestyle by providing opportunities for play and encourage sports or dance classes — make it a family affair!

Every fear faced, screen time managed, healthy meal enjoyed, and burst of physical activity is a step on their growth path. It is a path that's sometimes steep, sometimes winding, but always moving forward to new adventures. As you walk this path together, pause, appreciate the view, celebrate progress, and look forward to the exciting journey ahead. Remember, you're not just a parent; you are a guide, a companion, and a cheerleader every step of the way.

5.4 Navigating Everyday Challenges in the Elementary Years: A Practical Approach

Challenges	Practical Strategies
Tackling Fear and Anxiety	Consider your child's elementary years as a grand journey filled with challenges and opportunities akin to towering mountains and deep rivers. As your little explorer ventures into new territories, fears and anxieties may surface as formidable obstacles. To address this, providing a safe space for your child to openly express their feelings is crucial. Breaking down fears into manageable parts is a helpful strategy. Additionally, reassurance coupled with coping strategies, such as deep breathing or visualization can effectively manage anxiety.
Balancing Screen Time	While offering educational benefits, excessive screen time can lead to various issues. Maintaining a balanced digital diet, supported by setting screen time limits and monitoring content is crucial. Encouraging alternative activities, such as outdoor play and reading, helps in

Challenges	Practical Strategies
	providing a diverse set of experiences for your child.
Healthy Eating Habits	Your child needs a diverse and balanced diet. During the elementary years, the emergence of picky eating habits and unbalanced diets may occur. Including children in meal planning and preparation positively influences their dietary choices and attitudes towards food. Offering a variety of foods and encouraging experimentation helps in fostering healthy eating habits.
Encouraging Physical Activity	Physical activity is a cornerstone of a child's holistic development, impacting physical, cognitive, and emotional health. To foster an active lifestyle, provide opportunities for physical play and encourage participation in sports or dance classes. Model an active lifestyle by involving the whole family in physical activities, such as hikes, bike rides, or backyard games.

As we wrap up this chapter, let me share a heartwarming story from a dear friend, who like many of us, is steering through the rewarding yet challenging waters of the elementary years. Her son Alex (not his real name) was facing serious anxieties about starting a new school year.

In tackling Alex's fears, my friend created a safe haven for open conversations. She encouraged him to share his worries, breaking them down into smaller, manageable pieces. Together, they developed coping strategies, including deep breathing exercises and visualization techniques. As the school year progressed, so did Alex's confidence. The anxieties transformed into opportunities for growth. This personal journey mirrored the strategies discussed in this chapter: creating a nurturing environment, setting boundaries, involving the child in decision-making, and promoting healthy habits.

This story serves as a poignant reminder that the challenges we've explored aren't just theoretical; they play out in the lives of real families. With each practical step, we're not only deciphering the complexities of child development but also making a difference in the lives of children like Alex.

THE TEENAGE ENIGMA: 12 TO 19 YEARS

Welcome to the wild ride of the teenage years, where hormones are as unpredictable as the weather forecast.

In this chapter, we'll dive into the whirlwind of changes that define adolescence, a period of growth, self-discovery, and occasional eye-rolls that could rival a professional gymnast's routine.

Let me share a personal story to set the stage. My niece Sarah (not her real name) embarked on her teenage journey with the enthusiasm of an explorer setting out on a grand adventure. One day, I asked her about school, expecting the usual one-word response. To my surprise, she launched into a passionate monologue about her dreams, fears, and the intricate social dynamics of high school. As she spoke, I couldn't help but marvel at the complexity of the teenage experience. Sure, every one of us has been at this stage, but it is easy to forget how confusing it can be. Sarah was transforming from a curious child to a young adult, complete with dreams, dilemmas, and a newfound appreciation for sarcasm.

With that image in mind, let's unravel the fascinating layers of teenage brain development, hormonal roller coasters, and sleep patterns that challenge even the most resilient night owl.

Armed with understanding, empathy, and the occasional dose of humor, we'll navigate the maze of adolescence, making sense of the changes and ensuring our teens know they're not alone on this exhilarating journey.

Note: Risk-taking and decision-making take the forefront during this tumultuous yet transformative phase.

6.1 Teens and the Brain: Unraveling the Tapestry of Change

Adolescent Brain Development

Picture the brain as a garden, undergoing synaptic pruning and eliminating unused connections to shape and strengthen the remaining ones.

The *prefrontal cortex,* responsible for decision-making and impulse control, matures gradually during the teenage years, and during this process, teens learn to harmonize their thoughts, actions, and emotions. For example, they might struggle with impulse control, leading them to make impromptu decisions without fully considering the consequences. But this doesn't mean they are poor decision-makers; it's a natural process they really don't have control over.

Impact of Hormonal Changes on Behavior

The teenage journey is a roller coaster ride fueled by hormonal surges, characterized by loops of highs and lows. Testosterone and estrogen not only propel physical changes but also influence mood and emotions.

If you notice your child's usual calm demeanor transforming into a storm of emotions, blame it on the hormonal changes and try to understand what's going on in their bodies.

Sleep Patterns in Adolescence

Ever wondered why your teen is a night owl? Their biological clock undergoes a time zone shift during adolescence, making it challenging to synchronize with the early morning demands of school.

For them, it's like battling perpetual jet lag, struggling to align their body clock with the rhythm of daily life. This misalignment can result in insufficient sleep, affecting mood and academic performance.

Risk-taking and Decision-Making in Teens

Teenagers often gravitate towards risk, such as attempting daring feats or embracing last-minute exam preparation. During this time, the reward center of their brain is on overdrive, responding intensely to the thrill of risky behavior. Simultaneously, their decision-making skills are a work in progress, and impulsive decisions are a part of them. It's like they are driving with a powerful accelerator but an underdeveloped brake system.

Understanding these changes allows us to be co-pilots on their journey. We provide the right blend of freedom and guidance, set clear boundaries, offer unwavering support, and help them navigate the uncharted territory of adolescence.

As we do, we're not merely guiding them through this stage but nurturing the growth of confident, responsible, and resilient young adults.

6.2 Navigating the Teen Social Jungle

Hormones and mood swings are just the tip of the iceberg when it comes to the complicated world of teenagers. Behaviors, values, and identities can weigh them down and even be a significant cause of mood changes, breakdowns, and even serious mental health issues like anxiety and depression.

Here, peer pressure is the savvy salesperson, and your teen is the unsuspecting shopper.

Peer Pressure and Influence: Bargaining in the Teen Marketplace

Going by our marketplace analogy, peer pressure in the world of adolescents can feel like they are haggling over the latest trends and yielding to the persuasive voices of their peers. It's like buying the latest tech gadget - not because they need it, but because everyone else has one.

To help them outsmart peer pressure, give them a survival guide to the "marketplace." Encourage open conversations, teach them the art of saying "no," and explain the power of making informed choices.

Navigating Romantic Relationships

As your teen strolls through the marketplace, they might stumble upon the stall of romantic relationships. For teens, relationships are exciting and can consume them entirely. Remember your puppy love back in high school? It was intense, wasn't it?

While some relationships are a delightful mix of flavors, others are harder to swallow than an unexpectedly spicy dish.

Guide your teen through the romance section like a culinary expert explaining a menu. Discuss love ingredients and teach them about consent, respect, and healthy boundaries. Give them a crash course in relationship gastronomy - minus the indigestion.

But remember that this can be a touchy subject if, let's say, you don't really approve of their romantic choices. In such cases, tread carefully and keep in mind that the more you tell them no, the more they will want what you are saying no to – it's just teens being teens. Instead, try to reason with them from a logical point of view and let them make their own decision.

Role of Social Media: The Virtual Marketplace

Welcome to the digital age, where the marketplace extends into the virtual world of social media, which offers unending experiences, connections, and influences. Social media bombards your teen with tons of content, some beneficial, some not so much.

Help your teen navigate this virtual marketplace by discussing the potential risks and benefits, enabling them to make savvy choices. Encourage responsible social media use and teach them to question what they see online.

Importance of Real-life Social Interactions: The Heartbeat of the Marketplace

While the virtual world is a tempting convenience, real-life social interactions are the heartbeat of the marketplace. Face-to-face conversations, shared laughter, and communal experiences are vital for your teen's social development. In the end, they are more meaningful and real than what any virtual experience can offer.

So, urge your teen to engage in real-life social activities. Whether it's a family dinner, a hangout with friends, or a community event, these experiences enrich their social skills, empathy, and understanding of the world.

6.3 Navigating Conflict and Communication Barriers

Enhancing Communication Strategies

Communication is the bridge that connects you and your teenager, and if this bridge crumbles, it puts your relationship with your teen at risk.

It is crucial to employ effective tools and techniques to fortify this link, ensuring a constant and harmonious exchange of understanding.

Effectively communicating with your teenager involves not just hearing but actively listening, honestly expressing your thoughts, and responding with empathy.

Start by giving your teen your full attention when they speak, as if standing on this bridge, fully present, taking in the view. For instance, if your teen shares concerns about school, actively engage by asking follow-up questions or expressing understanding. When responding, honestly express your thoughts and feelings respectfully. Share your experiences, perhaps recalling a challenging situation from your own teenage years, to relate and empathize. Most importantly, validate your teen's feelings and demonstrate understanding, extending a metaphorical hand to help them cross the bridge without fear or hesitation.

Handling Teen Rebellion

At times, your teenager may exhibit rebellious behavior, challenging rules and asserting independence, akin to testing the bridge's strength by pushing against its boundaries. This rebellion is a natural part of adolescence, signifying their identity development and decision-making learning—a necessary test of their resilience.

To manage teen rebellion, consider setting clear and consistent boundaries while allowing some flexibility. For example, establish curfew times but allow room for negotiation based on responsible behavior. This approach reinforces the bridge's structure yet permits it to sway with the wind.

When addressing rule violations, maintain a calm demeanor and focus on the behavior rather than your teen. Share a personal experience of how learning from mistakes shaped your own growth.

6.4 Strategies for Conflict Resolution

Conflicts are inevitable in any relationship. How you manage these conflicts can either strengthen or weaken your relationship with your teenager.

One effective strategy is to use "I" statements instead of "you" statements, speaking from your perspective to express your feelings without blame or criticism.

For instance, instead of saying, "You always ignore my advice," rephrase it as "I feel unheard when my suggestions are not considered."

When conflicts arise, take a break if emotions run high. Share an example of how taking a step back and revisiting a conversation later helped resolve a disagreement in your own life so that they understand why you opt not to engage when emotions are high.

Most importantly, work towards a solution that respects both your and your teen's needs. Share stories of compromise from your own experiences, emphasizing the mutual benefits of finding common ground.

Understanding and Addressing Teen Privacy Needs

As your teenager grows, their need for privacy increases, resembling the construction of their own island at the other end of the bridge—a personal space to explore thoughts and feelings.

Respecting your teen's privacy is crucial to maintaining trust and fostering independence. For instance, give them space and time alone, respecting their closed bedroom door as their personal sanctuary.

Acknowledge their right to enjoy the island as their sole space, free from unnecessary intrusion.

However, it's also important to discuss the limits of this privacy and remind them of your parental responsibility. For example, agree on a visitation protocol for the island, ensuring their safety and well-being.

You can also share a personal story about how having open conversations about boundaries and privacy in your own life contributed to a healthy understanding within your family.

The teenage years present a winding road filled with peaks of joy, valleys of challenges, and a beautiful view of growth. As parents, we should be co-travelers on this journey, navigating alongside our teens with understanding, patience, effective communication, and respect for their privacy.

For a deeper understanding of the adolescent brain and behaviors, *visit www.JoyceTbooks.com,* where you can freely download the e-book titled "Adolescent Brain 101: A Crash Course for Parents and Educators to Navigate Teen Mental Development, Emotional Well-being, and Academic Success" using the keyword "mind" to unlock your complimentary gift.

THE BUILDING BLOCKS: NUTRITION FROM TODDLERHOOD TO ADOLESCENCE

When a plant is in its seedling stage, it requires different conditions to thrive than when it morphs into a fully-fledged tree. Equivalently, a child who is merely a toddler has different nutritional needs than those of your teen.

In this chapter, we will look at nutrition at every stage, beginning with toddlerhood.

7.1 Nutritional Needs of Toddlers

As your tiny tot transforms into a toddler, their nutritional needs set sail on a new course. Your toddler's diet should blend different types of food, as each food group plays a vital role in supporting their growth and development.

- Protein: Acts as the building blocks, essential for tissue repair and growth

- Fruits and vegetables: Contribute essential vitamins and minerals, providing a colorful and protective foundation.

- Grains: Provide the necessary energy to fuel their activities

- Dairy: Supplies essential nutrients for strong bones

In this phase of rapid growth, think of providing the right nutrition as laying down the bricks, one by one, building a castle that's not just strong but beautiful and uniquely your child's own. It's about understanding their nutritional needs, offering a feast of healthy foods, and setting the stage for lifelong healthy eating habits.

But remember that every little knight or princess is unique, and their nutritional needs might vary. You can seek the wise counsel of a pediatrician or a registered dietitian for personalized advice.

7.2 Healthy Eating Habits for Preschoolers and School-age Children

Preschoolers and school-age children will need a little extra since they use more energy daily than toddlers who are yet to join school.

For them:

- Carbohydrates: Will provide them with steady energy

- Proteins: Repairs tissues and support growth

- Water: Is vital for all body functions and for maintaining hydration

Fats: Offer long-lasting energy and aid brain development. Vitamins and minerals facilitate various bodily functions

But for this age, getting them to eat enough fruits and vegetables can be quite a challenge, considering that this is where they begin "choosing" foods.

Involve them in the food arts—grocery shopping and cooking! Let them pick a new vegetable, and let them stir the pot.

It is equally important to address their sweet cravings. While it's alright for your little one to enjoy the sweet treats occasionally, beware of potential health issues.

Offer naturally sweet foods like fruits and yogurt, and keep sweets as special treats so they remain enjoyable without becoming overwhelming. Promoting healthy eating habits is about teaching them the value of nutrition, helping them appreciate this, and empowering them to take control of their own health.

7.3 Meeting the Nutritional Needs of Teenagers

Teenagers experience a growth spurt that demands careful consideration of their nutritional needs. In this pivotal phase, **protein** emerges as paramount, tirelessly aiding in tissue repair and growth. It is crucial for the ongoing construction of their maturing bodies.

Ensure to include an array of animal and plant-based protein sources (remember, they get bored easily). Lean meats, poultry, fish, eggs, dairy products, nuts, seeds, and legumes are great examples.

Similarly, calcium is also essential. It plays a vital role in fortifying the bones and teeth – think of it as the solid steel beams upholding the structure. Dairy delights like milk, cheese, and yogurt are excellent calcium sources. Fortified plant-based milk or juices can serve as reliable substitutes for teens exploring dairy alternatives.

With teens, though, there's the tempting allure of fast food, possibly fueled by cravings, convenience, or what's "trending."

However, its high content of unhealthy fats, sugar, and sodium threatens the structural integrity of a teenager's health. Balancing this equation involves setting ground rules rather than an outright ban, perhaps reserving fast food as a weekly treat or for special occasions.

Encouraging healthier choices within the fast-food spectrum, like grilled instead of fried or water over sugary drinks, ensures a more stable foundation for their health.

Staying hydrated acts as the fundamental guide for various bodily functions, including digestion, nutrient absorption, and temperature regulation. Advocating for water consumption over sugary drinks supports the overall hydration blueprint.

Meanwhile, **physical exercise** complements nutritional efforts by maintaining a healthy weight, strengthening bones and muscles, and boosting mood and energy levels. Incorporating regular physical activity into a teenager's routine, whether through sports, dance classes, or daily walks, contributes significantly to their overall health blueprint.

Guiding teenagers in making the right choices may seem challenging. Still, armed with the right information, open communication, and leading by example, parents can help lay a robust foundation for a healthy life. Every meal, every snack, every glass of water, and every bout of exercise brings them one step closer to the towering castle of their potential.

Just be their trusty guide, and don't give up!

7.4 Overcoming Picky Eating and Other Challenges

Navigating the landscape of a child's dietary preferences involves employing strategic maneuvers, such as **introducing new foods gradually** and pairing them with familiar favorites. This gradual approach lets you add new foods while maintaining the comfort of the familiar.

Respecting a child's dislikes is crucial; forcing them to eat something they dislike can create a jarring experience. Instead, encourage them to try small amounts and acknowledge that it's okay if they don't immediately take a liking to a particular food. This lets kids test food while giving them the freedom to choose whether they want to continue eating it or not.

Certain foods can cause discomfort or even severe allergic reactions for some children. **Managing food allergies** requires educating children about the need to avoid allergenic foods. You can have a little board in their room indicating the foods they are allergic to so that they never forget.

Communicating with teachers, caregivers, and others who might feed the child is vital.

7.5 Family Meal Time

Family meals offer opportunities for connection and communication, setting a positive example for healthy eating habits.

Making family meals a regular occurrence, even if just a few times a week, establishes a routine that everyone anticipates and enjoys. During family meals, introduce new foods, discuss healthy eating habits, and share about each other's day.

Remember, the goal of family meals extends beyond nutrition to encompass social and emotional well-being. It's not about enforcing perfect table manners or serving gourmet dishes; instead, it's about relishing the joy of shared food, the warmth of togetherness, and the beauty of family love.

With eating habits covered, let's look a little into yet another essential factor in the development of kids — sleep.

THE LULLABY OF SLEEP: UNDERSTANDING AND MEETING SLEEP NEEDS AT DIFFERENT AGES

8.1 Understanding Sleep Needs at Different Stages

In the initial months of life, **newborns** sleep approximately 16 to 18 hours a day in 2 to 4-hour intervals. Their sleep pattern gradually shifts as they adapt to the world's day-night cycle, culminating in about 14 hours of sleep per day, including nighttime sleep and one to two naps, by the end of the first year.

The lullaby of sleep transforms as infants grow into toddlers. **Toddlers** aged 1 to 2 years require about 11 to 14 hours of sleep, accompanied by one or two daytime naps. As these young explorers transition into the **preschool age** of 3 to 5 years, their sleep needs decrease to about 10 to 13 hours a night, often bidding farewell to daytime naps.

School-age kids and adolescents introduce a new rhythm. Children aged 6 to 12 years thrive on 9 to 12 hours of nightly sleep, aligning with their active learning, play, and growth.

With their biological, academic, and social shifts, teenagers still require 8 to 10 hours of sleep per night. However, the "late-night syndrome" often clashes with early school start times, creating a unique challenge in this phase. In this case, you can give them tips on how to sleep better, such as minimizing caffeine, not using electronics near bedtime, avoiding afternoon naps (they love those), and maintaining a regular sleep-to-wake schedule.

Decoding these sleep needs involves recognizing the changes, making adjustments, and ensuring your kids get enough sleep based on their age.

8.2 Sleep Training Strategies for Infants and Toddlers

Crafting a bedtime routine for infants and toddlers is a tricky subject and will require you to have some patience so that you can reach the end goal – a restful night's sleep. This routine establishes predictability and security, signaling the transition to a calm, sleep-ready state.

Initiating the bedtime routine about 30 minutes before the usual sleep time prevents overtiredness, ensuring a harmonious start to the night. The key lies in consistency and timing.

Various sleep training methods cater to diverse parenting styles.

These methods are such as:

- The "cry it out" method, which involves allowing the child to cry for specified periods before offering comfort

- For those preferring a gentler approach, the "no tears" method functions like a soothing ballad, with more parental involvement and a gradual reduction of dependence.

- The "fading" method entails decreasing parental presence until the child can sleep independently.

Recognizing that each child is unique underscores the importance of finding the right rhythm and melody that resonates with them.

These strategies not only address sleep issues but also impart valuable skills such as self-soothing and independence. Night wakings are normal for infants and toddlers. Encouraging self-soothing by waiting a few minutes before responding and providing minimal interaction can allow them to resume sleep independently.

Through these sleep training strategies, parents resolve sleep-related challenges and instill crucial skills in their children. A consistent sleep schedule also contributes to a child's overall health, development, and well-being.

8.3 Addressing Sleep Problems in School-age Children and Teens:

Restoring the Symphony of Sweet Dreams

As children progress from infancy to adolescence, encountering unexpected disruptions, such as nightmares, night terrors, and insomnia, becomes a part of the process. Understanding these interruptions and implementing appropriate strategies can help restore the soothing rhythm of restful sleep for school-age children and teens.

Nightmares and Night Terrors

Imagine a serene lullaby, its harmonious flow suddenly interrupted by a discordant note—a nightmare or night terror jolting your child from peaceful slumber. These nocturnal disturbances, while unsettling, can be understood and addressed to restore the tranquility of your child's sleep.

Nightmares are basically scary dreams, often occurring during the second half of the night when there's more rapid eye movement (REM) sleep, associated with vivid dreams.

When your child experiences a nightmare, they'll likely remember the dream and may seek comfort. Offering reassurance, acknowledging their fear, and soothing them back to sleep is paramount to restoring harmony.

On the other hand, night terrors are characterized by intense fear, shouting, thrashing, or even sleepwalking, with no recollection of the event in the morning.

Ensuring your child's safety is crucial during a night terror, but avoiding waking them is advised. There's usually no need to discuss it in the morning since they're unlikely to remember the episode.

Managing Screen Time Before Bed

In the digital symphony of today's world, screens play a dominant role. However, just before bedtime, their stimulating effects can disrupt the soothing rhythm of the sleep lullaby. The blue light emitted by screens can interfere with the production of melatonin, the hormone that regulates sleep.

To manage screen time before bed, establishing a digital curfew is crucial. Turning off all devices at least an hour before bedtime sets the mood for sleep time.

Encourage relaxing pre-sleep activities like reading a book, drawing, or taking a warm bath.

Addressing Insomnia in Teens

Sometimes, sleep can remain elusive despite the sweetest lullaby and the most serene environment. Insomnia, characterized by difficulty falling asleep, staying asleep, or waking up too early, can be a significant issue during adolescence.

If your teen struggles with insomnia, it's crucial to identify any potential causes. These could include stress, anxiety, depression, or lifestyle factors like caffeine consumption or lack of physical activity. Trace insomnia back to its source to understand what's causing the disruption.

Encourage good sleep hygiene, including consistent sleep-wake times, a quiet sleep environment, and avoidance of stimulating activities before bed. If insomnia persists, seek help from a healthcare professional.

8.4 The Impact of Sleep on Development and Behavior: Unveiling the Magic of Rest

In your child's development, sleep plays a pivotal role. The impact of sleep extends far beyond physical rest, influencing cognitive development, emotional regulation, and even physical health.

Let's understand these benefits in depth.

Sleep and Cognitive Development

Consider sleep as a magical key that unlocks your child's cognitive potential. As they close their eyes and drift into dreamland, their brains switch gears, processing the information gathered during the day, consolidating memories, and building neural connections. It's like their very own secret workshop, humming with activity while the rest of the world is asleep.

Complex cognitive processes take place during sleep. For example, information is transferred from the hippocampus, where it is temporarily stored, to the cortex, where it becomes part of long-term memory.

Therefore, ensuring your child gets sufficient sleep can directly impact their academic performance. Think of it as providing them with a magical toolbox filled with cognitive tools that can support their learning, creativity, and problem-solving abilities.

Sleep and Emotional Regulation

How do you feel when you've had just a few hours of sleep? Groggy and moody, right? Similarly, lack of sleep can make it harder for your child to manage their emotions, react appropriately to situations, and cope with stress – and for them, it's more intense than it is for an adult!

Research has shown that sleep-deprived children may be more prone to mood swings, irritability, and anxiety.

Ensuring your child gets the sleep they need gives them a sturdy foundation that empowers them to navigate their emotional seas with greater skill and resilience.

Sleep and Physical Health

Think of sleep as a powerful potion, brimming with restorative powers that rejuvenate your child's physical health. Adequate sleep is essential for various bodily functions, including growth and immune response.

During sleep, the body releases growth hormones, which help children grow and support muscle mass and repair cells and tissues.

Sleep also plays a crucial role in appetite regulation. It helps balance the hormones that make your child feel hungry (ghrelin) or full (leptin). If your child doesn't get enough sleep, their ghrelin levels go up, and their leptin levels go down, which could make them feel hungrier than when they're well-rested.

By prioritizing sleep, you're not just ensuring your child gets their beauty sleep; you're also fortifying their physical health, supporting their growth, and promoting overall well-being. It's like gifting them an elixir that can boost their health and happiness.

So, as we finish off this chapter, let's commit to providing our children with the sleep they need to grow, learn, and thrive. After all, a well-rested child is a happy, healthy, and successful child. Although the symphony of sleep may have different movements, it all plays together to create a beautiful melody of health and well-being.

NAVIGATING THE DIGITAL LANDSCAPE: SCREEN TIME AND ITS IMPACT ON CHILD DEVELOPMENT

As we traverse this digital landscape, our first stop is understanding the impact of screen time on your child's development. From cognitive growth and social skills to physical health, let's delve into how screen time could shape your child's developmental journey.

9.1 The Impact of Screen Time on Development: Navigating the Digital Landscape

Screen Time and Cognitive Development

Imagine your child's mind as a garden, each interaction, each experience, a seed that grows into a tree of knowledge. When used mindfully, screen time can be like a gentle rainfall, nurturing these seeds and promoting cognitive development. Educational games can foster problem-solving skills, interactive stories can enhance language abilities, and digital art tools can stimulate creativity.

However, excessive screen time can lead to cognitive overstimulation. Research suggests that excessive screen time can impact children's attention span, memory, and learning abilities. It's like the garden is so flooded that new seeds can't take root properly.

For instance, a study published in JAMA Pediatrics found that higher levels of screen time at ages 2 and 3 were associated with poorer performance on developmental screening tests at ages 3 and 5. This emphasizes the need for a balanced approach to screen time, ensuring it's a gentle rain, not a storm in your child's cognitive garden.

Screen Time and Social Skills

Picture your child in a playground, engaging in lively games, sharing toys, and resolving conflicts. These interactions are crucial for developing social skills, much like a rehearsal for a choir performance. But what happens when the rehearsal time is cut short because of excessive screen time?

While digital platforms can offer interactive experiences, they cannot fully replicate the nuances of face-to-face interactions. Non-verbal cues like body language, tone of voice, and facial expressions are not as easily conveyed or interpreted on digital platforms. It's like trying to perform a choir piece without being able to see or hear the other singers.

A study published in the journal "Computers in Human Behavior" found that sixth-graders who went five days without exposure to technology were significantly better at reading human emotions than kids with regular access to phones, televisions, and computers.

This suggests that excessive screen time might be like a mute button on the choir performance, making the melody of social interactions less vibrant.

Screen Time and Physical Health

Screen time is a sedentary activity usually involving sitting on a comfortable couch (unless your child is dancing to some rhyme tunes).

While it might be enjoyable and relaxing, too much time on the couch can lead to physical health concerns. It can impact your child's physical fitness, posture, and even their vision. When your child spends a significant amount of time engaged in screen activities, it often cuts down on the time spent on physical activities like running, jumping, or even simple tasks like walking. This lack of physical activity can potentially lead to childhood obesity, a growing concern in many parts of the world.

Additionally, prolonged screen time often means sitting or slouching in front of the screen for extended periods, which can lead to poor posture and associated musculoskeletal problems.

Lastly, staring at screens for long hours can strain your child's eyes, leading to problems like dry eyes, blurred vision, and headaches.

As we navigate the digital landscape, understanding the impact of screen time on your child's cognitive development, social skills, and physical health is crucial. It's about maintaining the balance on the tightrope, harnessing the benefits of the digital world, and mitigating the risks. Use screen time like a tool, not a trap, and empower your child to grow, learn, and thrive in an increasingly digital world.

9.2 Guidelines for Healthy Screen Use: Navigating the Digital Tightrope

In the digital era, guiding your child through the noisy streets of screen time can be challenging. But with clear guidelines, a focus on active engagement, and designated screen-free zones and times, you can ensure a healthier and more balanced digital diet. It's about teaching your child to savor the digital dessert mindfully, to enjoy the sweetness without overindulging.

Setting Screen Time Limits

Having clear guidelines about screen time can help your child develop responsible digital habits. When setting these limits, consider factors like your child's age, individual needs, and daily routine. A two-year-old will have different screen time needs than a twelve-year-old.

Encourage your child to engage in other important activities like homework, reading, physical play, and family time before they enjoy their digital dessert. In other words, promote a balanced meal before the sweet treat.

Encouraging Active Screen Time

Screen time can be passive or active. Passive screen time often involves merely consuming content, like watching videos or scrolling through social media. Active screen time, on the other hand, engages your child's mind more meaningfully, like writing a blog post, creating digital art, or playing an educational game.

Promoting active screen time is like encouraging your child to help bake the dessert. They're not just consuming but also learning, creating, and actively participating. Active screen time can provide opportunities for learning and skill development. For instance, coding games can foster problem-solving skills, digital art platforms can enhance creativity, and educational apps can support academic learning.

9.3 Using Technology for Learning

Educational Apps and Websites

Multiple apps and websites offer a wealth of resources to support your child's academic learning. They feature interactive lessons, quizzes, and games that make learning engaging and fun.

For instance, apps like Khan Academy and Duolingo or websites like National Geographic Kids and Starfall provide a range of resources for various subjects, catering to different age groups and learning styles.

Online Tutoring and Courses

As your child advances in their academic journey, they might encounter challenging trails or steep climbs. Online tutoring and courses are like experienced guides, providing personalized assistance and in-depth knowledge to help your child overcome these challenges.

Online tutoring offers the advantage of one-on-one instruction tailored to your child's pace and needs. It's like having a personal guide, offering step-by-step assistance and immediate feedback. Platforms like Chegg Tutors, Wyzant, or Skooli connect your child with qualified tutors across various subjects, making finding the right guide for their academic journey easier.

Online courses, on the other hand, offer comprehensive coverage of a topic or a subject. Websites like Coursera, Udemy, or EdX provide a range of courses, from programming languages to creative writing, calculus, and environmental science. These are like detailed guidebooks, providing a wealth of information for your child to explore at their own pace.

Virtual Reality in Education

Imagine if your child could step into the past to witness a historical event or shrink down to explore the inner workings of a cell. Virtual Reality (VR) in education makes this possible. It's like a magical portal, transporting your child to different places, times, and scales, providing an immersive and interactive learning experience.

VR can transform abstract concepts into tangible experiences, aiding understanding and retention. For instance, exploring the solar system in a VR environment can make the lessons on planets and space more engaging and memorable for your child.

While VR technology is still emerging, platforms like ClassVR or Google Expeditions are making strides in bringing VR-based learning to the classroom and beyond. It's like the next-generation compass, map, or even a spaceship, redefining the boundaries of learning and exploration.

Integrating technology into learning can transform your child's educational experience, making it more engaging, personalized, and effective. With educational apps and websites, online tutoring, and virtual reality, the digital landscape offers a rich array of tools to support your child's learning journey.

So, let's encourage our children to embrace these digital tools instead of other mindless digital uses.

9.4 Addressing Cyberbullying and Online Safety

Signs of Cyberbullying

Cyberbullying, the digital cousin of traditional bullying, involves the use of electronic communication to bully a person, typically by sending intimidating or threatening messages. It's like a graffiti artist defacing the city walls with hurtful words and images; in this case, the wall is social media apps and websites.

So, how can you tell if your child is encountering cyberbullying on their digital wall? Look out for changes in your child's behavior or mood after using the internet or a digital device. They might appear upset, anxious, or reluctant to discuss what they're doing online.

Your child might also start avoiding social interactions, both online and offline, or display an unusual interest or disinterest in their digital devices.

Online Privacy and Safety Tips

In the digital city, safeguarding your child's online privacy is more like teaching them the rules of the road and guiding them to navigate safely and responsibly.

Here are a few tips to help your child protect their privacy in the digital realm:

- Personal Information: Teach your child not to share personal information like their full name, address, or phone number online. Ask them to treat their personal information like their home keys – they would give those to a random stranger, now would they?

- Strong Passwords: Encourage them to use strong, unique passwords for their online accounts. It's akin to having a sturdy door lock so no one can bypass their home.

- Privacy Settings: Help them understand and use the privacy settings on their social media accounts and apps. It's like drawing the curtains in their home, keeping any prying eyes away.

- Friend Requests: Remind them to only accept friends or follow requests from people they know in real life. After all, they can only invite trusted and known friends into their home.

Responding to Cyberbullying

If your child encounters cyberbullying in their digital city, it's crucial to respond appropriately. Here's how:

- Open Communication: Encourage your child to talk to you or another trusted adult about the incident.

- Document Evidence: Instruct your child to take screenshots or printouts of the bullying messages or posts.

- Report and Block: Help your child report the bullying to the social media platform or website. Also, guide them to block the person who is cyberbullying them.

- Seek Professional Help: If the cyberbullying continues or if your child is distressed, seek help from a counselor, psychologist, or law enforcement agency.

In the bustling metropolis of the digital world, cyberbullying is a significant concern, casting a shadow over it. By understanding the signs of cyberbullying, safeguarding online privacy, and responding effectively to cyberbullying, we can equip our children to navigate the digital city safely and confidently.

In the next chapter, we'll look into how to support our children who are abled differently.

EMBRACING UNIQUENESS: UNDERSTANDING AND SUPPORTING CHILDREN WITH SPECIAL NEEDS

10.1 Recognizing Early Signs of Developmental Delays: Embracing Uniqueness

In the first part of this chapter, we will focus on recognizing early signs of developmental delays. We'll explore certain milestones to look out for, discuss signs of Autism Spectrum Disorder (ASD), and delve into the indicators of Attention Deficit Hyperactivity Disorder (ADHD).

Developmental Milestones

Imagine if you're out on a road trip without a route map, unsure of which landmarks to look out for. In the journey of child development, milestones serve as these crucial landmarks, indicating typical skills or behaviors exhibited at certain age stages.

For instance, by six months, most babies can roll over in both directions. By one year, they may be attempting to walk. And by two years, they might start to speak in two to three-word sentences. These milestones are like signboards along the road, guiding you on your child's growth journey. However, suppose a child consistently fails to reach these milestones within an expected timeframe. In that case, it might be an early sign of a developmental delay.

Signs of Autism Spectrum Disorder

Children with ASD (Autism Spectrum Disorder) often have distinct behaviors, and recognizing these early signs can lead to earlier diagnosis and intervention.

For instance, babies with ASD might avoid eye contact, have difficulty with back-and-forth play, or not respond to their names by 12 months. They may also show repetitive behaviors, like flapping their hands, rocking their body, or spinning in circles.

Signs of ADHD

Children with ADHD (Attention Deficit Hyperactivity Disorder) often exhibit signs of inattention, hyperactivity, and impulsivity, which can interfere with their functioning or development.

For instance, they might have difficulty sustaining attention in tasks, be easily distracted, fidget often, or make impulsive decisions. Recognizing these early signs requires you to tune into their unique melody, understand their rhythm, and acknowledge their place in the process of child development. It's the first step towards appreciating their uniqueness, advocating for their needs, and supporting their growth and development.

10.2 Parenting Children with Autism, ADHD, and Other Conditions

Behavior Management Strategies

As a parent of a child with Autism, ADHD, or any other condition, your role is much the same. You're guiding your child, helping them navigate their unique behaviors and responses. Navigating behavior management strategies can be challenging, but with patience, understanding, and the right approach, you can help your child manage their behaviors harmoniously.

One effective strategy involves **clear and consistent communication.** You need to communicate your expectations to your child. Use simple and direct language, and ensure your instructions are understood.

Positive reinforcement is another powerful tool. Reward your child for their positive behaviors, whether with praise, attention, or tangible rewards.

Structure and routine can also provide your child with a sense of security and predictability. Establish a consistent daily routine for meals, homework, playtime, and bedtime.

Supporting Social Skills Development

When it comes to developing social skills, consider it as learning the language of social interaction. For children with Autism, ADHD, or other conditions, this language might not come naturally. As a parent, you can play a crucial role in helping your child learn this language.

Modeling appropriate social behaviors is a fundamental strategy. Show your child how to make eye contact during conversations, use polite language, and share toys during playdates.

Role-playing can also be a useful tool. It's like practicing a musical piece before a performance. Use dolls, puppets, or even yourselves to act out social scenarios. Practice greetings, turn-taking, expressing feelings, and resolving conflicts.

Lastly, provide plenty of **opportunities for social interaction**. Set up playdates, involve your child in group activities, and encourage participation in social events.

Working with Therapists and Teachers

In this development ensemble, therapists and teachers play a crucial role in offering guidance, support, and companionship.

- Therapists can provide specialized strategies tailored to your child's needs. Working closely with therapists can help you understand your child better and equip you with effective strategies for managing behaviors, fostering social skills, and supporting learning.

- Teachers, on the other hand, interact with your child in a different setting - the school. Collaborating with teachers can provide valuable insights into your child's academic and social performance.

- Maintaining open communication with therapists and teachers can ensure that everyone is in sync, playing the same symphony. Regular meetings, progress reports, and home-school notebooks can facilitate this communication.

Parenting a Child with Special Needs

Parenting a child with Autism, ADHD, or other conditions is always a learning experience, with every day bringing new insights. With effective behavior management strategies, support for social skills development, and collaboration with therapists and teachers, you can guide your child and foster growth, development, and well-being.

However, it's not just about managing behaviors or developing skills; it's about embracing their uniqueness, appreciating them, and celebrating their place in the grand symphony of life.

10.3 Supporting Learning in Children with Special Needs

Individualized Education Plans (IEP)

The Individualized Education Plan (IEP) is crafted to fit your child's unique learning style. It is a detailed blueprint outlining specific learning goals and the support/services the school will provide to help your child achieve these goals.

The process of developing an IEP is a collaborative effort between educators, school psychologists, speech and language therapists, and, most importantly, you as parents. Your role is crucial, offering valuable insights into your child's strengths, challenges, interests, and needs.

Once implemented, the IEP is not a static document and may need periodic analysis to gauge what still works and what needs adjustment. This will ensure the plan fits your child perfectly even as they grow and learn.

Assistive Technology in Learning

In the realm of special education, assistive technology acts as a magic toolbox filled with tools designed to transform and enhance your child's learning experience. These tools bridge the gaps created by specific learning deficits.

Assistive technology ranges from simple, low-tech tools like highlighters and pencil grips to high-tech devices like text-to-speech software and electronic worksheets.

For instance, speech recognition software can transcribe spoken words into written text if your child struggles with writing. Similarly, a text-to-speech tool can bring words to life for a child who finds reading challenging.

Integrating these tools into your child's learning process unlocks doors to learning and empowers your child to explore new realms of knowledge and skills.

Inclusive Education

An inclusive classroom is a supportive and accommodating environment where your child learns alongside their peers. Teachers implement effective teaching strategies tailored to diverse learning needs, ensuring all students can access the curriculum.

Inclusion is not solely about academic benefits; it's a transformative experience fostering social and emotional development. Children build relationships, gain an understanding of diversity, and develop empathy. Inclusive education signifies that every child, irrespective of abilities or disabilities, has the right to learn, grow, and succeed in a regular classroom.

Supporting learning in children with special needs involves a multi-faceted approach: tailoring education plans (IEP) to fit unique needs, using assistive technology to make learning accessible, and embracing inclusive education to value uniqueness and recognize potential.

10.4 Navigating the Special Education System

Understanding Special Education Laws

Special education laws provide rights and protections to children with disabilities and their parents.

Two paramount laws govern special education in the United States: the Individuals with Disabilities Education Act (IDEA) and Section 504 of the Rehabilitation Act.

IDEA mandates that public schools serve the educational needs of eligible students with disabilities, ensuring the right of way for their learning journey. It guarantees every eligible child a Free and Appropriate Public Education (FAPE) in the Least Restrictive Environment (LRE). Section 504 ensures equal access to education, acting as a rule against discrimination. Children may receive accommodations and modifications in the general education classroom.

Understanding these laws equips you with the knowledge needed to navigate the special education system effectively.

Advocating for Your Child

As a parent, you are the most dedicated advocate for your child. Your role in the special education process is vital, from identifying your child's needs to planning their Individualized Education Program (IEP) and ensuring its proper implementation.

Begin by learning everything about your child's specific condition. Familiarize yourself with special education laws and understand them for an informed and smoother ride. Open communication with teachers, therapists, and the school administration is crucial.

Advocating for your child ensures they receive the support and services needed for success, steering them through learning journey roadblocks.

Navigating the special education system may seem complex but armed with a clear understanding of special education laws, a strong advocacy for your child, and effective collaboration with the school team, you can help your child navigate this road more smoothly. While the journey may have its share of bumps and turns, remember that every mile covered is a mile closer to your child's success.

10.5 Embracing Diversity Beyond The Classroom

Fostering an Inclusive Environment

Building on the concept of inclusive education, fostering an inclusive environment extends beyond the classroom. It's about creating a society that embraces and supports the diverse needs of every child.

Parents, teachers, and community members play vital roles in fostering inclusivity. This involves promoting empathy, understanding, and acceptance. Encouraging children to appreciate differences and learn from one another contributes to a nurturing environment where every child feels valued.

Nurturing Emotional Well-Being

Child development goes beyond academic achievements; emotional well-being is equally significant. For children with special needs, navigating the social landscape can be challenging. Thus, creating an emotionally supportive environment is essential.

Parents and educators can encourage open communication about emotions. Teaching all children to express themselves, understand their feelings, and empathize with others fosters emotional intelligence. This emotional support contributes to a positive atmosphere where children can thrive, not just academically but also emotionally.

NURTURING RESILIENCE: THE ART OF TURNING SETBACKS INTO COMEBACKS

Think of resilience in children like a rubber band. Life stretches them, pulls them in different directions, and twists their experiences. But with resilience, they can bounce back stronger, ready for the next challenge and this chapter will show how you can help them build this necessary quality.

11.1 The Role of Failure in Building Resilience

Teaching Growth Mindset

Imagine your child facing a challenging puzzle. Instead of giving up, what if they see it as an opportunity to learn and grow? That's a growth mindset – the belief that abilities and intelligence can improve with effort. It's like viewing a puzzle not as a wall but as a ladder; each failed attempt is a step closer to the solution.

Cultivating a growth mindset involves praising your child's effort, not just their intelligence. For example, say, "I'm impressed by your persistence and hard work!" This shift reinforces that effort and persistence lead to growth and improvement.

Encouraging Risk-Taking

Picture a toddler taking their first steps. They stumble and fall but eventually learn to walk. Encouraging your child to take risks – try new activities, make decisions – fosters resilience. It's like urging the toddler to stand up and walk, even if they might stumble.

Ensure these risks are age-appropriate and safe, creating a secure environment. It's like providing the toddler with a soft carpet, reducing the impact of a fall as you encourage them to try again.

Responding to Failure

Let's say your child gets a low test grade. Here, your response can either make or break them. Instead of focusing on the grade, discuss what they learned. It's the same way you would focus on the toddler's effort to walk, not the times they stumbled.

Responding with empathy, optimism, and encouragement helps your child see failure as a learning opportunity. It's about helping them understand that everyone makes mistakes, everyone fails, and that's okay – it's how we learn and grow.

11.2 Strategies for Fostering Resilience

Building a Strong Support Network

For your child to grow mentally, they need support. A robust support network serves as your child's stake and protective net, providing support, protection, and a safe space.

This network includes family, friends, teachers, coaches, and mentors. Each should offer emotional support, guidance, encouragement, and a safe space for your child.

Family members provide a stable environment filled with love, care, and understanding. Much like a protective net, friends offer companionship, shared experiences, and a sense of belonging. Teachers, coaches, and mentors guide your child, encourage their interests, and inspire them to reach their potential, much like the sun and rain that nourish the tree.

Teaching Coping Skills

Life will always come with its set of challenges. It's a path with rocks and thorns and can never be in a straight line. Teaching coping skills is like giving your child sturdy shoes, a map, and a compass to navigate this path.

Coping skills help kids manage stress, overcome obstacles, and bounce back from setbacks. There are various techniques for this that you can teach your child, including deep breathing, positive self-talk, taking a walk, meditation, and self-soothing tactics.

For instance, deep breathing can help your child calm their racing heart before a big test, much like a pair of comfortable shoes can ease the journey on a rocky path. On the other hand, positive self-talk can boost their confidence during a challenging task.

Encouraging Independence

Independence fosters self-confidence, self-reliance, and resilience in children. Start with small tasks appropriate for their age, gradually introducing more complex ones.

Remember, the goal isn't to push them into the sky unprepared but to equip them with the skills and confidence to spread their wings and fly. It's about watching them take their first flight, tumble, get up, and try again until they're soaring high.

11.3 Teaching Problem-Solving Skills

Guided Problem-Solving

Think of guiding your child through problem-solving like gently nudging a curious puppy. Discuss a problem, brainstorm solutions, evaluate, choose a solution, and make a plan.

The goal is to empower them to think critically and make sound decisions, not to solve their problems for them.

Role-Playing Scenarios

Role-playing scenarios allow your child to rehearse problem-solving in a safe setting. Identify a challenging scenario, discuss solutions, act it out, and review.

It provides a safe space to practice problem-solving, gain confidence, and prepare for real-life situations.

Encouraging Creative Thinking

Encourage your child to think creatively when faced with a problem. Prompt them to ask "What if?" questions and explore different approaches.

This fosters innovative thinking, transforming problems into opportunities for learning and growth.

Encouraging creative thinking can empower your child to see problems as opportunities to innovate, create, and learn.

In conclusion, building resilience in children involves teaching a growth mindset, encouraging risk-taking, responding to failure positively, creating a strong support network, teaching coping skills, fostering independence, and developing problem-solving skills. Each strategy contributes to nurturing a resilient child, ready to face life's challenges with confidence.

One Step, One Stumble, One Comeback at a Time

As we explore how to build resilience in children, it's crucial to appreciate that resilience is an ongoing journey. The strategies mentioned are interconnected, creating a beautiful dance of development and growth.

While sometimes they may stumble, the point is not to give up on them. Even as adults, sometimes things can get overwhelming, and our resilience may take a back seat, especially during difficult times. In such times, they'll need all the support they can get from you.

11.4 Supporting Children During Difficult Times

Navigating Difficult Conversations with Your Child

Imagine your child standing at the edge of a deep pool, uncertain about taking the plunge. Discussing difficult topics with your child can evoke a similar apprehension. These topics might include death, divorce, illness, or distressing world events. It's like standing hand-in-hand with your child at the pool's edge, unsure of how to navigate the conversation.

Creating a Safe Space for Conversation

The first crucial step is to establish a safe and comfortable space for the dialogue. Much like finding a quiet spot by the pool, choose a location free from distractions where your child feels secure.

Speak in a calm and gentle manner, using simple and straightforward language suitable for your child's age and emotional maturity. It's akin to explaining how to jump into the pool, where to aim, and how to float, ensuring they grasp the information.

Encourage your child to express their feelings and concerns. Validate their emotions and reassure them that feeling upset, scared, or confused is okay. Similar to acknowledging their fear of the deep water, validate and comfort them.

Remember, the goal is not to push your child into the pool of difficult topics but to guide them so they can take the plunge when they feel ready. When they do, they'll discover they can navigate the issue with confidence and resilience.

Providing Emotional Support

Visualize your child struggling to stay afloat in the deep pool — splashing, kicking, gasping for breath. Offering emotional support during challenging times is akin to throwing them a flotation device, ensuring they stay afloat, and reassuring them they're not alone.

Listen to your child with empathy and understanding. This conveys that you're there for them.

Offer comfort and reassurance. Remind your child that it's okay to feel upset, and these emotions will pass. This is comparable to shouting encouraging words to a swimmer, boosting their morale.

Encourage your child to use coping strategies like deep breathing or engaging in a comforting activity. Just as reminding the swimmer of their lessons encourages them, support your child in utilizing strategies to navigate emotional waves.

Remember, emotional support is not about rescuing your child from the pool but providing them with tools and confidence to swim through emotional waves independently.

Be their lifeguard, ready to intervene if needed, while also cheering them on as they learn to navigate on their own.

Seeking Professional Help

Sometimes, despite your best efforts, your child might struggle in the deep pool. Sometimes, they might need more than a flotation device or swimming tips – they might need a professional swim coach. Similarly, when your child continues to grapple with difficult emotions or situations, it might be time to seek professional help.

A mental health professional, such as a psychologist or counselor, can offer targeted strategies and therapies to help your child manage emotions and cope with challenging situations. This is analogous to hiring a professional swim coach with the expertise to assist struggling swimmers.

Don't hesitate to seek help if your child's emotional distress is severe, prolonged, or interferes with daily activities. Seeking professional help is not a sign of weakness; it's a step toward resilience and a testament to your commitment to your child's emotional well-being. Let this be known to them as well.

Navigating the Deep Pools of Life

Supporting your child during difficult times involves discussing challenging topics, providing emotional support, and seeking professional help when necessary. It's about standing by their side as they navigate the deep waters of life, offering a reassuring presence, a helping hand, and a listening ear. It ensures that no matter how deep the pool is, your child never feels out of their depth.

EMOTIONAL ABCS: NAVIGATING THE SEAS OF FEELINGS AND RELATIONSHIPS

As a mother and a writer, I've come to appreciate the profound impact emotions have on our lives. This chapter will explore the intricate world of emotional intelligence, drawing parallels between understanding and deciphering emotions.

For you to teach your child about their emotions, you need to be attuned to yours first.

12.1 Understanding Emotions: The Basics of Emotional Intelligence

Identifying Emotions

Imagine entering a market blindfolded, relying solely on the sounds surrounding you. Motherhood often feels like this — navigating through the myriad of emotions, unsure of the origin or intensity. Identifying emotions requires tuning into your inner world, much like listening to your child's laughter or acknowledging the tired sighs after a challenging day.

The first step is to remove the blindfold, pause, and recognize these emotions without judgment. Understanding your child's emotional landscape starts with acknowledging their feelings.

Understanding the Causes of Emotions

Removing the blindfold in the market reveals a vivid scene — a fruit seller calling out prices, a florist engaged in conversation, and a child crying over a dropped ice cream. Suddenly, the chaos makes sense.

Similarly, understanding the causes of our emotions unveils the intricate tapestry of our experiences. In motherhood, a rough day at work may be more than just professional challenges. It could be the weight of piled-up responsibilities, a difficult conversation with a colleague, or simply feeling overwhelmed.

Peeling back these layers allows us to connect with our emotional landscape.

Recognizing Emotions in Others

As a writer, I'm attuned to the subtle nuances of language, both spoken and unspoken. Recognizing emotions in others involves a similar attentiveness. In the market, voices and cues become familiar – the fruit seller's enthusiasm, the florist's warmth, or the child's cries of distress.

Similarly, recognizing emotions in our loved ones requires an understanding of their verbal and non-verbal cues. For example, a quiet friend avoiding eye contact during our coffee catch-up may signal a need for empathy and support.

This understanding equips us with the tools to navigate our emotional seas effectively, fostering healthier relationships within ourselves and with those we love.

12.2 Strategies for Teaching Emotional Regulation

Deep Breathing and Relaxation Techniques

Navigating the emotional landscapes of motherhood often feels like crossing a vast desert. Deep breathing becomes a simple yet potent oasis in this journey.

Teaching your child to take slow, deep breaths. This gives them a moment to pause, refresh, and regain composure. Incorporating visual imagery, such as imagining breath as waves or wind, makes this practice even more effective, so don't be afraid to be creative.

As a mother, I've often found solace in these moments, not just for my child but for myself, in the quiet interlude of a shared breath.

Using Art and Play to Express Emotions

As a writer, I understand the power of expression through various mediums. These mediums act as redirections to release otherwise difficult-to-express feelings. Encouraging your child to draw or paint their emotions can provide them with a canvas to articulate the nuances of their feelings.

Play, another powerful medium, can provide a space for your child to enact scenarios, mirroring their emotions through toys and stories.

Simply base your child's mode of expression on their age, personality, and preferences.

Teaching Self-Soothing Techniques

In the tempest of emotions, we all seek an anchor. Just as a sailor steadies their ship, kids learn to navigate the emotional seas, maintaining calm amidst the storm when they grasp self-soothing techniques.

These activities, such as listening to calming music and cuddling a soft toy, become a sanctuary from the raging emotional storms. However, as with other qualities, teaching emotional regulation is an ongoing narrative that will require constant practice to master.

Next up, let's explore how to foster empathetic and caring children.

12.3 Nurturing Empathy: The Art of Perspective Taking

Teaching Perspective-Taking

Perspective-taking, a crucial aspect of empathy, teaches your child to see the world from different viewpoints. As a parent, your role in this process is pivotal.

Guide your child to consider the feelings of others and help them foster a broader understanding of the human experience. Engage in honest discussions with them. Books, movies, and real-life situations can offer unique perspectives on emotions and humanity.

Real-life situations serve as the proving ground for this skill. When a friend is upset, I guide my child to consider the possible causes, encouraging them to empathize by imagining themselves in their friend's position.

Narratives can also help kids step into the characters' shoes, comprehend their emotions, and see things from a perspective they otherwise wouldn't have. Bedtime stories will work well for younger children, and for older kids, you can get them an inspirational novel.

Encouraging Kindness and Compassion

As a mother, I encourage my child to nurture kindness and compassion through thoughtful words and actions. Helping a friend, sharing toys, or offering a kind word fosters an environment where empathy blossoms.

It's not just about teaching empathy; it's about cultivating a way of being, a disposition towards kindness that becomes second nature.

Aim to model acts of kindness in your home. Your child observes and absorbs these gestures, understanding that empathy isn't a theoretical concept but a living, breathing force that shapes our connections.

Kids model what they see us do, so to nurture these values, you must exemplify them first.

Role-Modeling Empathy

Emotional intelligence is a craft, and empathy is its fine art. Ideally, I always try my best to ensure that my gestures, words, and responses are the tools that shape my child's understanding. Express empathy towards your child, precisely acknowledging their feelings, much like a craftsman molding clay.

In every interaction with others, showcase the beauty of empathy through kindness, understanding, and patience.

Remember that nurturing empathy is a collaborative effort between you and your child – with you being at the forefront.

12.4 Strategies for Teaching Empathy: A Mother's Perspective

Using Everyday Moments as Teaching Opportunities

I've come to realize that everyday moments provide rich soil for sowing the seeds of empathy. From sharing a meal to playing in the park, these are the moments where empathy can be exemplified.

During conflicts or disagreements, I guide my child to consider the feelings of others involved. One question that helps me do this is asking, *"If you were in their shoes, how would you feel?"*

This prompts them to take a step back and view the situation from the other person's perspective.

Encouraging Open Communication

Encouraging open communication is essential in fostering empathy. Try to create a space where your child feels safe to express their feelings and thoughts. This open dialogue serves as a bridge, connecting you and your child through shared understanding and deepening the roots of empathy.

Cultivating a Culture of Empathy

Again, for any quality to become second to nature, you have to help your child realize this by showing them it's not a one-time thing – it's part of your home.

I consciously cultivate an environment where empathy is celebrated. This involves acknowledging and validating emotions and teaching my kids that vulnerability is not a weakness but a strength. This empathy culture should extend beyond your home to how they engage with the world.

In moments of conflict, it also calls for you to understand that your child's perspective is valid and worthy of acknowledgment. Extend empathy to them as well.

12.5 Nurturing Empathy - A Compassionate Voyage

Acts of Kindness and Compassion

As a family, we cultivate a habit of kindness any chance we get. Baking cookies for neighbors, donating to local shelters, or expressing gratitude through simple gestures become rays of sunshine, warming the garden of relationships surrounding us.

Encouraging my child to extend compassion during tough times is crucial to this journey. Whether through a listening ear, comforting words, or silent companionship, these acts of compassion help them enhance empathy.

Acknowledging and reinforcing these acts of kindness becomes an essential part of the process. Expressing pride in your child's efforts reinforces the positive impact of their actions, creating a cycle of empathy that thrives on acknowledgment and encouragement.

As they learn to navigate the waters of emotions and relationships, they become skilled sailors and empathetic lighthouses, guiding others with their understanding, kindness, and compassion.

12.6 Nurturing Emotional Expression

This chapter will explore the intricacies of encouraging emotional expression in children and teens. To get the point home, we'll draw parallels between the nuanced world of emotional landscapes and nature's favorite singers – birds.

The Safe Nest: Creating a Space for Emotions

Imagine your home as a cozy nest, inviting every emotion to take flight and be acknowledged without reservation. Much like bird feeders and birdbaths attract a variety of birds, open conversations at home create an environment that beckons all emotions. These conversations form the foundational structure of the emotional nest, where every emotional flutter is embraced, every chirp of joy celebrated, and every melancholic song acknowledged.

Ensuring that responses to a child's emotions mirror the watchful guardianship over a bird aviary is crucial. Regardless of the emotional melody—be it a cheerful chirp or a mournful song—the response should remain supportive and understanding.

The Song of Validation

Validating a child's emotions involves accepting their feelings as genuine and significant, much like appreciating the authenticity of a bird's song. When a child shares their emotional turmoils, responding with statements acknowledging their feelings becomes a form of emotional validation.

As you acknowledge their emotions, it is important to do this without attempting to fix their problems or dismiss their significance. All they need at the moment is a listening ear.

Encouraging Emotional Literacy

Emotional literacy serves as the birdwatcher's guidebook, helping children accurately identify and express their emotional flock. Beginning with basic emotions as the familiar birds in their habitat, you play the role of the guide introducing these emotional companions.

Visualize this process as familiarizing your child with the most common bird species, with emotions being the varied birds in their emotional landscape.

As children grow, their emotional vocabulary expands, mirroring the thrill of discovering new bird species in a diverse forest. More complex emotions become part of the repertoire, allowing children to navigate the intricate nuances of their emotional landscape easily.

Everyday situations and media serve as the bird-watching expedition, where children spot different emotional birds and learn to recognize their unique songs..

Fostering Emotional Expression

Creating an environment that fosters emotional expression is like nurturing a bird-friendly habitat. In this habitat, every emotion is welcome, whether it's a big bubbling scar emotion or a chipper one.

It's about transforming feelings from adversaries into allies, from elusive ghosts into reliable guides, and from distressing miseries into valuable messages.

By doing so, we cultivate a world where emotional expression is not only accepted but celebrated—an invaluable skill that empowers children to navigate the seas of feelings and relationships with confidence.

Reflecting on Our Emotional State

As this chapter concludes, let's take a moment to reflect on our own feelings. To help our kids handle their emotions better, we must first be in control of our own. So, don't shy away from digging deep and assessing your own emotional landscape.

In the next chapter, you'll learn how to create a strong relationship with your child and what it takes to get here.

See you there!

PARENTING STRATEGIES FOR EVERY AGE

13.1 The Power of Positive Parenting

Using Positive Reinforcement

When your child displays a behavior you wish to encourage, respond with praise, attention, or a reward. For instance, if they spontaneously help a sibling tidy up spilled toys, you might express, "I noticed how you assisted your sister without being asked. That was very kind and helpful of you. Great job!"

Focusing on Strengths

Every child possesses unique strengths, be it kindness, curiosity, creativity, or perseverance.

Make a habit of recognizing and appreciating these strengths. If your child has a talent for storytelling, you could say, "I love listening to your stories! You have such a creative imagination." Focusing on strengths can enhance your child's self-confidence, motivating them to leverage these qualities in various situations.

Building Self-Esteem

To foster your child's self-esteem, offer genuine, specific praise that centers on their effort and progress rather than just the outcome. Instead of a generic "You're the best soccer player," you might say, "I've noticed how hard you've been practicing your kicks, and it's really paying off in the games!"

Additionally, involve your child in tasks and responsibilities that promote competence and confidence, such as setting the table or caring for a pet. Always applaud their efforts and express confidence in their abilities.

Nurturing a Beautiful Relationship

With positive reinforcement, you nurture the behaviors you want to see more of. Focusing on strengths highlights the vibrant threads that make your child unique. And through building self-esteem, you strengthen your child's sense of self-worth and resilience.

As we delve further into this parenting journey, let's recognize that every thread matters, and each element of parenting, whether it be love, discipline, communication, or patience, plays a crucial role in creating an overall design.

13.2 Nurturing a Strong Relationship: From Infancy to Adolescence

Spending Quality Time Together

Imagine the parent-child relationship as a garden, evolving from the early days of infancy to the complexities of adolescence. From the moment of birth, your time and attention become the nourishing sunlight crucial for the growth of the delicate seedling.

During **infancy**, your baby craves simple acts like cuddling, singing lullabies, or just gazing into their eyes. These moments are like the morning sunlight warming the seedling and inviting it to grow.

As your child evolves into a **toddler** and preschooler, quality time might involve playing games, reading stories, or engaging in creative activities together.

In the **school years and adolescence**, shared hobbies, meaningful conversations, and family traditions become vital for continued growth. Even as your teenager seeks independence, they still need the warmth of your time and attention, much like a mature plant needs sunlight.

Remember, quality time is about the connection, not the quantity. It's not about extravagant outings but about being fully present, engaged, and connected during these shared moments. It's about providing the sunlight that nurtures your relationship, helping it grow, flourish, and bloom.

Maintaining Open Communication

In the garden of your relationship, communication serves as the water, essential for survival and growth. From the coos and gurgles of infancy to the complex conversations of adolescence, maintaining open communication is key to a strong relationship.

During infancy, your baby communicates through sounds, facial expressions, and body language. Responding to these cues with warmth and consistency builds a foundation of trust and understanding, much like regular watering helps establish a young plant.

As your child's communication skills develop, encourage open and honest conversations. Listen to their thoughts, validate their feelings, and express your own honestly. It's like watering the plant regularly, ensuring it gets the right amount of moisture it needs to grow.

Communication might become more challenging during adolescence as your teenager seeks independence and privacy. Respect their need for privacy but also keep the lines of communication open. It's like adjusting the watering schedule for a mature plant, providing just the right amount it needs.

Remember, open communication is not just about talking; it's also about listening, understanding, and validating. It's about providing the water that nourishes your relationship, ensuring it stays healthy and continues to grow.

Showing Unconditional Love

Unconditional love serves as the nutrient-rich soil in the garden of your relationship. It's the assurance that, no matter what happens, your love for your child remains constant and unwavering. From their first breath, your baby needs this unconditional love, much like a seedling needs a secure base from which to explore the world.

As your child grows and begins to navigate the world, they will make mistakes, face challenges, and experience failures. Through all of this, your unconditional love provides the assurance that they are loved for who they are, not for their achievements or behaviors. It's like the nutrient-rich soil supporting the plant, providing nourishment, and anchoring it firmly.

In adolescence, as your child seeks their identity and independence, your unconditional love becomes a safe space for them to explore, experiment, and express themselves. It's a nurturing environment that allows them to blossom into their unique selves.

But keep in mind that showing unconditional love is not about accepting inappropriate behaviors or neglecting discipline. It's about separating the behavior from the child and reassuring them that your love for them is unwavering and constant.

13.3 Using Age-Appropriate Language and Active Listening Techniques

Using Age-Appropriate Language

Imagine yourself as a storyteller on the radio, addressing a diverse audience ranging from toddlers to teenagers. To captivate each listener, you adjust your language to be accessible and engaging for every age group. This is akin to using age-appropriate language in your parent-child communication.

For **toddlers**, your language needs to be simple, concrete, and filled with repetition, much like playing nursery rhymes on the radio—easy to follow and enjoyable for your little listener.

As your child grows into a **preschooler**, you can introduce more complex language, longer sentences, and more abstract ideas. It's like transitioning from nursery rhymes to children's stories—a bit more complex but still engaging and understandable.

School-age children can comprehend more complex sentences and engage in meaningful conversations. You can discuss ideas, ask open-ended questions, and use metaphors or analogies, much like discussing a favorite book or movie—engaging and thought-provoking.

During the **teenage years**, your child can understand adult language, grasp abstract concepts, and engage in deep, thoughtful discussions. You can discuss complex issues, share personal experiences, and debate ideas.

Active Listening Techniques

Active listening is an essential skill, whether you're hosting a radio show or navigating the intricate landscape of parent-child communication. It involves giving your child your full attention, free from distractions, much like focusing on the caller's voice on the radio, undisturbed by background noise.

It's about showing interest and understanding through your body language, gestures, and facial expressions. Lean in, nod along, and mirror your child's emotions to convey your engagement.

Another aspect of active listening is reflecting on what your child is saying and feeling. It's like summarizing the caller's story on the radio, ensuring you've captured the essence correctly.

Most importantly, active listening is about resisting the urge to jump in with advice or solutions. Hold back your opinions and give your child the space to express themselves. Fight the urge to interrupt, allowing them to complete their story.

Non-Verbal Communication

Your tone of voice is a powerful tool that can convey a range of emotions and messages. A soft, warm tone conveys love and understanding, while a sharp, loud tone might convey anger or frustration. It's like the music you play on your radio show, setting the mood for your listeners.

Facial expressions and body language also speak volumes. A smile, a nod, or a hug can convey love, approval, and comfort. Conversely, a frown, a stern look, or crossed arms might convey disapproval, anger, or distance.

Your actions are equally potent as a form of non-verbal communication. They can either reinforce your words or contradict them. Consistency between your words and actions is crucial. It's like ensuring your radio show's content matches its title and description, maintaining credibility and trust among your listeners.

Active listening calls for you to reach out to your child, tune into their frequency, and communicate with love, understanding, and respect.

13.4 Balancing Friendship and Authority as a Parent

As parents, finding this balance is easier said than done, and we often find ourselves leaning into one side more than the other. But finding balance is crucial for the well-being of your child.

Setting Clear Boundaries

Setting clear boundaries is like drawing a map for your child, marking out safe zones, danger zones, and points of interest. It gives them a sense of security and understanding of what's expected of them.

Clear boundaries could encompass screen time limits, bedtime routines, or expectations for respectful behavior. It's about defining the playground where they can run free, the areas where they need to be cautious, and the zones where they are not allowed to venture.

But it's important to understand what boundaries aren't. Setting boundaries isn't about restricting your child's freedom but about ensuring their safety and well-being. It's about providing a map not to limit their exploration but to guide them on their adventure.

Being Consistent with Rules

Being consistent with rules reinforces boundaries and makes your expectations clear and predictable. Consistency could involve maintaining the same consequences for a particular behavior, sticking to established routines, or upholding the same rules across different situations.

Being consistent doesn't mean being rigid or inflexible. It's about providing a steady pattern while allowing adjustments where necessary.

Showing Respect and Understanding

Respect involves acknowledging your child's feelings, valuing their opinions, or honoring their individuality. Understanding entails empathizing with your child's experiences, struggles, and triumphs.

Showing respect and understanding isn't about agreeing with your child all the time but about validating their experiences and emotions.

Respect also involves respecting your child's privacy, space, and individuality (letting them be themselves).

Balancing Friendship and Authority

It's a delicate balance, knowing when to be a friend, sharing in the joy and laughter, and when to be an authority, providing structure and guidance. This balance evolves as your child grows, and it shifts with situations. Some will require you to be exclusively a friend and others the authority, while some will require a little bit of both.

NOTE: if it's something that can put them in harm's way, don't be afraid to take the friendship cap off and approach the situation as the authority figure.

CHAPTER 14

THE POWER OF PLAY: A KEYNOTE TO CHILD DEVELOPMENT

14.1: The Power of Play in Child Development

Picture this: a toddler engrossed in a game of peek-a-boo, an elementary-age child building an intricate Lego castle, or a teenager lost in an immersive video game.

What do these scenes have in common?

They all involve play, an activity often associated with fun and enjoyment. But play is not merely child's play; it's a powerful catalyst for child development. It's like the hidden track on an album, often overlooked but adding depth and richness to the whole composition.

Play and Cognitive Development

Let's take the example of a preschooler playing with blocks. They stack, align, and perhaps knock them down with a giggle. This simple play activity is a cognitive workout in disguise.

As they manipulate the blocks, they develop their spatial reasoning skills, understanding shapes, sizes, and how they relate to each other. It's like a mini architect exploring the principles of design and structure.

Moreover, play enhances problem-solving skills. Consider a child trying to fit a square peg into a round hole. After several unsuccessful attempts, they figure out it just won't work. They find the square hole, and voila - the peg fits! This is problem-solving in action, facilitated by play. It's like a mini detective cracking a case through trial and error.

Play and Social Development

Play also serves as a social classroom for children. Think of a group of children involved in a pretend play scenario. They run a pretend restaurant, assign roles, follow the rules, negotiate, and cooperate.

These social interactions during play help children learn how to cooperate, resolve conflicts, and understand social norms. It's like a rehearsal for a play, with each child learning their part, understanding the script, and synergizing with others.

Moreover, playing games with rules, such as board games or sports, teaches children about fairness, taking turns, and honor. It's like being in a mini democracy, learning to abide by rules, respect others' rights, and accept outcomes gracefully.

Play and Emotional Development

Play also has a significant role in children's emotional development. Have you noticed how children often reenact scenarios through their play, like going to the doctor or dealing with monsters? This type of play helps them process their experiences, understand their emotions, and gain a sense of control. It's like a mini therapy session, helping them make sense of their world and their feelings.

Further, imaginative play allows children to express their emotions and learn to regulate them. For instance, a child might express their fear of monsters by acting out a story where they bravely defeat the monster. This play narrative helps them manage their fear and builds their courage.

The science of play reveals its profound impact on cognitive, social, and emotional development. It's the keynote to child development, setting the tone for growth, learning, and well-being.

So, let's value play, facilitate it, and celebrate it as a fundamental right of every child – whenever possible, opt for it over any other form of entertainment.

14.2 Choosing Age-Appropriate Toys and Games

Toys for Infants and Toddlers

Let's imagine you're in a toy shop, standing in the aisle marked 'Infants and Toddlers.' The shelves are filled with colorful toys, each trying to catch your eye. But which one to choose? Let's see.

At this stage, infants are exploring the world through their senses. So, sensory toys like rattles, soft toys, teething toys, and musical toys are great choices. These toys offer a variety of textures, sounds, and colors for your little one to explore. Toys such as a soft teddy bear, a rattling ball, or a teething ring offer the double benefit of keeping your baby entertained while stimulating their sensory development.

As your baby grows into a toddler, their play becomes more active and imaginative. Toys that encourage physical coordination and cognitive skills are ideal at this stage. Think of stacking blocks, shape sorters, or push-pull toys.

These toys stimulate your toddler's problem-solving skills, hand-eye coordination, and motor skills. It's like setting up a mini gymnasium for your toddler, filled with fun and learning.

Toys for Preschoolers and School-age Children

Now, let's move to the next aisle, labeled 'Preschoolers and School-age Children.' As children grow older, their play evolves, becoming more complex and social. The toys they play with should reflect this evolution.

Preschoolers enjoy pretend play, so toys that stimulate their imagination are perfect. Dollhouses, kitchen sets, doctor sets, or costumes can lead to hours of imaginative play. It's like giving them a magic wand, transforming the living room into a castle, a jungle, or a spaceship!

Toys that promote cognitive development, creativity, and social skills are ideal for school-age children. Consider a complex puzzle, a creative craft kit, or an intriguing science experiment set - these toys challenge your child's mind, stimulate their creativity, and often require cooperation with others.

Toys for Teens

Finally, let's not forget the teens. Though they might no longer play with traditional toys, many 'toys' still cater to their interests and developmental needs.

Strategy games, intricate puzzles, or construction sets can provide intellectual stimulation for teens. They require concentration, strategic thinking, and patience. It's like inviting them to a chess match, a battle of wits, and a test of patience.

Art and craft sets, musical instruments, or digital design software can cater to your teen's creative side. They provide an outlet for self-expression and can lead to the development of lifelong hobbies. It's like giving them a blank canvas, a set of paints, and the freedom to create their masterpiece.

In conclusion, selecting age-appropriate toys and games for your child is like curating a personalized playbox for them. It's about understanding their developmental needs, catering to their interests, and providing opportunities for fun and learning. So, let's choose wisely, play merrily, and make the most of the power of play!

14.3 The Benefits of Outdoor Play

Physical Health Benefits

Outdoor play encourages children to be active, promoting their physical fitness and motor skills. Running, jumping, climbing, or playing ball games get their heart pumping, their muscles working, and their body moving. It's like a natural workout routine, fun and invigorating.

Furthermore, outdoor play exposes children to sunlight, an excellent source of vitamin D. This essential nutrient helps the body absorb calcium and phosphate from our diet - nutrients crucial for healthy bones, teeth, and muscles. It's like nature's magic potion, fortifying their body and fueling their growth.

Cognitive and Emotional Benefits

Outdoor play stimulates children's curiosity and imagination. Whether it's a bug on a leaf, the shapes in the clouds, or the hidden world of a mud puddle, the outdoor environment is full of wonders that pique their curiosity and fuel their imagination. It's like an open-ended storybook, each page with intriguing characters and fascinating stories.

Moreover, outdoor play provides opportunities for children to manage risks and face challenges, fostering their resilience and self-confidence. Activities like climbing a tree, balancing on a log, or jumping from a height all involve risk assessment, decision-making, and overcoming fear. It's like a mini adventure course, each obstacle a lesson in courage and determination.

Furthermore, outdoor play can have a calming effect on children. The soothing sounds of nature, the warmth of the sunlight, or the feel of grass under their feet can be therapeutic, reducing stress and fostering emotional well-being.

Social Benefits

Outdoor play encourages social interaction as children engage in cooperative play, negotiate rules, and resolve conflicts. Whether it's a team sport, a make-believe game, or a playground activity, these interactions foster communication skills, cooperation, and empathy.

Moreover, outdoor play promotes inclusion and diversity. Children of different ages, abilities, and backgrounds come together in the park or playground, learning to accept and appreciate differences.

But even the most active explorer needs some downtime. Let's see how to navigate this.

UNRAVELING THE MAGIC OF DOWNTIME: EMBRACING BOREDOM AND FREE PLAY IN A BUSY WORLD

Picture a serene lake – calm, reflective, surrounded by stillness. Now, think of this lake as your child's mind during downtime. In our busy world, we often overlook the power of these moments, rushing from one scheduled activity to another.

But in these quiet moments, the magic of creativity, self-reflection, and imagination truly comes alive.

15.1 The Importance of Downtime and Boredom

Embracing Creativity

What if we hit pause for a moment? What if we let our kids experience the luxury of downtime, free play, and, yes, even boredom? I know boredom might sound surprising, but bear with me!

Transforming Stillness into Creativity

Boredom might seem unexciting at first, but it's a playground for creativity. Research even shows that boredom fosters problem-solving skills. So, next time your child says, "I'm bored," see it as an opportunity for them to unleash their creativity.

Encouraging Free Play

Free play is another gem. It's like a playground for your child's mind, where they lead, create their own rules, and build confidence.

It's the space where they explore, experiment, and express themselves without any restrictions.

15.2 Strategies for Managing Over-Scheduling

Balancing Scheduled Activities and Free Time

Now, it's all about finding the right balance between scheduled activities and free time. While structured activities have their perks, free time nurtures creativity and self-reflection.

You can create a schedule that accommodates both without overwhelming your child.

Prioritizing Activities

First up, prioritizing activities! Evaluate each one based on its value to your child's development and well-being. Rank them in order of priority to create a harmonious composition. It's not about cramming in as many activities as possible; it's about creating a balanced schedule.

Setting Realistic Expectations

Set realistic expectations within your child's skill level. Consider your child's age, energy levels, and personality. It's about creating a schedule that gets them excited and willing to follow it.

Allowing for Flexibility

Flexibility is key! Life is unpredictable, and so is childhood. Be ready to adapt to changes and leave room for unstructured time. Remember that the mind and preferences of a child can change in an instant, and you have to be ready to accommodate and adjust to keep the schedule effective.

15.3 Finding Balance: School, Play, and Rest

Now, let's talk about balancing school, play, and rest.

Imagine a seesaw: school on one side, play on the other, and rest in the center. The goal is to keep it balanced. Set a regular schedule for school and homework, carve out time for play (both structured and free), and ensure there's ample time for rest.

— Encouraging a Variety of Activities

Encourage various activities, like painting a rainbow in your child's life. Academic, physical, creative, social, and solitary activities each add their unique hue to your child's development.

A good night's sleep is crucial, but don't forget about moments of rest throughout the day. These give your child time to reset briefly during the day (daytime rest is more important for toddlers and preschoolers).

15.4: Nurturing the Present - Cultivating Mindfulness in Children and Teens

Imagine standing at the edge of open water, the water's surface perfectly mirroring the clear blue sky. Now imagine this scene as a representation of mindfulness - the ability to be fully present, aware of where we are and what we're doing, and not overly reactive or overwhelmed by what's going on around us.

As adults, we often hear about the benefits of mindfulness, from stress reduction to improved focus. But what about children and teens? Can they, too, benefit from mindfulness? The answer is a resounding yes!

Mindfulness Activities for Children

Think of a kaleidoscope, with its array of colorful patterns that shift and change with each turn. Mindfulness activities for children are like this kaleidoscope, offering a variety of ways to engage their attention and focus.

— Spidey Sense

One simple mindfulness activity for children is the "Spider-Man" exercise. Ask the child to pretend they are Spider-man, using their "spidey senses" to tune into what they can hear, see, smell, taste, and touch in the present moment. This activity helps children connect with their senses and focus on the here and now.

— The Breath of Calmness

A simple mindful breathing exercise for children is the "teddy bear" practice. Ask your child to lie down and place a teddy bear on their belly. Instruct them to take slow, deep breaths, noticing how the teddy bear moves up and down with each breath. This visual cue can make the practice more engaging and tangible for young children.

For older children and teens, the "4-7-8" breathing technique can be effective. This involves inhaling for a count of 4, holding the breath for a count of 7, and exhaling for a count of 8. Regular practice of this technique can help reduce stress, promote relaxation, and enhance focus.

Encouraging Mindful Eating

Another activity is the "mindful eating" exercise. The next time your child eats a snack, encourage them to look at it, touch it, smell it, and taste it slowly, savoring each bite. This practice of eating with attention and appreciation can transform this routine activity into a mindful moment.

— Flavorful Awareness

Mindful eating involves paying full attention to the experience of eating without any distractions. It's about noticing the food's colors, smells, textures, and flavors. It's about eating slowly, savoring each bite, and listening to the body's hunger and fullness cues.

Encouraging mindful eating can start with simple practices. For instance, you can start a meal with a moment of gratitude, appreciating the food and the efforts that brought it to the table. You can also have "device-free" meals, encouraging everyone to focus on their food and each other.

— Fostering a Deeper Connection with Food

Encouraging mindful eating fosters a deeper connection with food and subsequently a healthier relationship with eating.

As you help your child to become more mindful, join them in the practice to make it more fun and let them learn directly from you – after all, you are their best (and favorite) teacher!

CONCLUSION

Dear parent, we are finally at the end of our incredible journey together. From the wonders of prenatal development to the rollercoaster ride of toddlerhood and through the peaks and valleys of the teenage years, we've navigated the vast landscape of child development, gathering a treasure trove of knowledge and insights along the way.

Louise Hart's quote, *"The Golden Rule of Parenting is to do unto your children as you wish your parents had done unto you,"* encapsulates a fundamental principle of parenting rooted in empathy and self-reflection.

The quote draws parallels with the well-known Golden Rule, which suggests treating others as you would like to be treated. In the context of parenting, it encourages you to consider the kind of upbringing you wish you had and extend that same kindness, understanding, and support to your own children.

The quote implies that you may carry memories and experiences from your own childhood, both positive and negative. By reflecting on what you wished for in terms of parental care and guidance, as a parent you can consciously incorporate those positive elements into yor own parenting approach.

This approach emphasizes a cycle of positive behavior and nurturing, aiming to break any negative patterns that might have been experienced in one's own upbringing.

In essence, the quote encourages parents to be mindful of their actions and decisions, considering the impact they may have on their children. It underscores the importance of fostering a loving and supportive environment that promotes your child's emotional, social, and cognitive well-being.

Ultimately, by adhering to this "Golden Rule of Parenting," you strive to create a positive legacy that shapes not only your children's lives but potentially the way those children, when grown, will parent future generations.

A Journey Through the Ages

Remember when we explored the importance of a balanced diet during the embryonic and fetal stages? Or the fascinating adventure of cognitive growth during the preschool phase? How about the strategies we unearthed for handling the unique challenges of adolescence? And let's not forget the magical power of play, the joy of downtime, and the soothing rhythm of mindfulness.

Every stage and chapter brims with valuable lessons and practical strategies, like a compass guiding us through the wild terrain of parenting.

The Transformative Power of Knowledge

Through this journey, we've discovered the transformative power of knowledge. Understanding child development isn't just about knowing the facts and figures. It's about gaining a deeper insight into your child's world, seeing the world through their eyes, and appreciating the magic of their growth.

It's like unlocking a secret language, a language that allows you to communicate with, understand, and guide your child in a way that respects their unique journey.

Putting Strategies into Practice

Now, armed with this knowledge, it's time to put the strategies into practice. Remember, there's no 'one-size-fits-all' approach to parenting. Use these strategies as a starting point, a guide. Adapt them to your child's needs, your family dynamics, and your parenting style. Try them out, see what works, make mistakes, learn, and adjust.

Cherishing Each Moment

Parenting is not a race to the finish line; it's a fascinating journey filled with beautiful moments, challenging experiences, and invaluable lessons.

It's about growing together, learning together, and loving unconditionally. So, as you continue your journey, remember to cherish each moment, celebrate each milestone, and embrace each challenge with love, patience, and understanding.

A Salute to Parents

I want to leave you with this final thought as we part ways: You are doing an amazing job. Yes, you! Parenting is no easy feat, and there will be days when you question yourself and feel overwhelmed. But remember, you are not alone. You are part of a community, a tribe of parents, all navigating this journey together.

And now, with this book, you have the power of knowledge, a toolkit of strategies guided by a heart full of love.

Here's to the Journey

So here's to you, to your child, and the incredible journey of parenting. Here's to the laughter, the tears, the triumphs, and the trials; here's to the beautiful process of child development that shapes humanity!

Keep learning, keep loving, and keep being the amazing parent you are. The journey continues, and I can't wait to see where it takes you.

BOOK THOUGHTS & OPINIONS

Dear Readers,

I am writing to express my deepest gratitude for your support in reading my book. Your time and engagement mean the world to me. If you've enjoyed the journey through these pages, please consider leaving a review. Your words can guide and inspire other readers, helping them discover the book and decide if it's the right fit for them.

Reviews are the lifeblood of independent authors, and your honest feedback can make a significant impact. Thank you for being a part of my literary journey, and I look forward to hearing from you.

To submit a review, kindly navigate to your Order History, locate the book in your purchased items, and select 'Write a Product Review.'

With gratitude,

Joyce T.

Bonus Gift

As a gesture of gratitude, I'm delighted to offer you a complimentary copy of the e-book Bundled 2-in-1, aimed at enhancing your understanding of your child. This resource offers a comprehensive exploration of child development, spanning from embryo to teen.

Adolescent Brain 101 + Simplifying Child Development 2-in-1

A Stage-by-Stage Guide to Nurturing a Healthy
Child's Mind from Embryo to Teen
Scan QR code to download with Access Code: mind

www.JoyceTbooks.com

REFERENCES

Stages of Prenatal Development | Lifespan Development. (n.d.). Retrieved from https://courses.lumenlearning.com/suny-hvcc-lifespandevelopment4/chapter/prenatal-development/

Article Author(s). (Year). Maternal healthy lifestyle during early pregnancy and ... [Article Title]. Retrieved from https://www.ncbi.nlm.nih.gov/pmc/articles/PMC6179147/

National Institute of Diabetes and Digestive and Kidney Diseases (NIDDK). (Year). Health Tips for Pregnant Women. Retrieved from https://www.niddk.nih.gov/health-information/weight-management/healthy-eating-physical-activity-for-life/health-tips-for-pregnant-women

Business Insider. (Year). OB-GYN Doctors Debunk the 25 Biggest Pregnancy Myths. Retrieved from https://www.businessinsider.com/ob-gyn-

doctors-biggest-pregnancy-myths-debunked-
2019-10

Centers for Disease Control and Prevention (CDC).
(n.d.). Infants (0-1 years). Retrieved from
https://www.cdc.gov/ncbddd/childdevelopment/
positiveparenting/infants.html

Centers for Disease Control and Prevention (CDC).
(n.d.). Breastfeeding Benefits Both Baby and Mom.
Retrieved from
https://www.cdc.gov/nccdphp/dnpao/features/b
reastfeeding-benefits/index.html

HelpGuide. (n.d.). Building a Secure Attachment Bond
with Your Baby. Retrieved from
https://www.helpguide.org/articles/parenting-
family/building-a-secure-attachment-bond-with-
your-baby.htm

MedlinePlus. (n.d.). Common Infant and Newborn
Problems. Retrieved from
https://medlineplus.gov/commoninfantandnewbo
rnproblems.html

Children's Minnesota. (Year). Developmental
milestones 2 to 3 years. Retrieved from

https://www.childrensmn.org/educationmaterials
/childrensmn/article/15312/developmental-
milestones-2-to-3-years/

Hello VaiA. (n.d.). Theories of Language Acquisition:
Differences & Examples. Retrieved from
https://www.hellovaia.com/explanations/english/
language-acquisition/theories-of-language-
acquisition/

Mayo Clinic. (Year). Potty training: How to get the job
done. Retrieved from
https://www.mayoclinic.org/healthy-
lifestyle/infant-and-toddler-health/in-
depth/potty-training/art-20045230

Mayo Clinic. (Year). Temper tantrums in toddlers:
How to keep the peace. Retrieved from
https://www.mayoclinic.org/healthy-
lifestyle/infant-and-toddler-health/in-
depth/tantrum/art-20047845

American Academy of Pediatrics. (n.d.).
Developmental Milestones: 3 to 4 Year Olds.
Retrieved from
https://www.healthychildren.org/English/ages-

stages/preschool/Pages/Developmental-
Milestones-3-to-4-Year-Olds.aspx

Raising Children Network. (n.d.). Creative activities
for preschooler learning and development.
Retrieved from
https://raisingchildren.net.au/preschoolers/devel
opment/creative-development/preschooler-
creative-activities

Mom Life Made Easy. (n.d.). 10 Essential Skills For
Pre-k or Kindergarten Readiness. Retrieved from
https://momlifemadeeasy.com/preschool-
kindergarten-readiness/

LA Parent. (Year). 7 Preschool Problems and Tips on
How to Solve Them. Retrieved from
https://www.laparent.com/7-preschool-
problems-and-tips-on-how-to-solve-them/

Harvard Medical School. (n.d.). Screen Time and the
Brain. Retrieved from
https://hms.harvard.edu/news/screen-time-brain

Brookings. (Year). New evidence of the benefits of
arts education. Retrieved from

https://www.brookings.edu/articles/new-evidence-of-the-benefits-of-arts-education/

Lesley University. (n.d.). 6 Ways Educators Can Prevent Bullying in Schools. Retrieved from https://lesley.edu/article/6-ways-educators-can-prevent-bullying-in-schools

Harvard Health Publishing. (n.d.). The adolescent brain: Beyond raging hormones. Retrieved from https://www.health.harvard.edu/mind-and-mood/the-adolescent-brain-beyond-raging-hormones

U.S. Department of Health and Human Services. (n.d.). Social Media and Youth Mental Health. Retrieved from https://www.hhs.gov/surgeongeneral/priorities/youth-mental-health/social-media/index.html

Verywell Family. (Year). 8 Essential Strategies for Raising a Confident Teen. Retrieved from https://www.verywellfamily.com/essential-strategies-for-raising-a-confident-teen-2611002/

Empathic Parenting Counseling. (n.d.). Teenage Rebellion: Effective Ways to Handle It at Home.

Retrieved from
https://empathicparentingcounseling.com/bondin
g/teenage-rebellion-and-ways-to-handle-it/

Centers for Disease Control and Prevention (CDC).
(n.d.). Infant and Toddler Nutrition. Retrieved from
https://www.cdc.gov/nutrition/infantandtoddlern
utrition/index.html

U.S. Department of Agriculture. (n.d.). USDA MyPlate
Nutrition Information for Preschoolers. Retrieved
from https://www.myplate.gov/life-
stages/preschoolers

American Academy of Pediatrics. (n.d.). A Teenager's
Nutritional Needs. Retrieved from
https://www.healthychildren.org/English/ages-
stages/teen/nutrition/Pages/A-Teenagers-
Nutritional-Needs.aspx

Parents. (Year). 13 Proven Strategies for Picky Eaters.
Retrieved from
https://www.parents.com/recipes/nutrition/pick
y-eater-strategies/

National Institutes of Health. (Year). Children's sleep
linked to brain development. Retrieved from

https://www.nih.gov/news-events/nih-research-matters/children-s-sleep-linked-brain-development

Sleep Foundation. (n.d.). Sleep Training: Definition & Techniques. Retrieved from https://www.sleepfoundation.org/baby-sleep/sleep-training

Sleep Foundation. (n.d.). Sleep Disorders in Children. Retrieved from https://www.sleepfoundation.org/children-and-sleep/sleep-disorders-in-children

Article Author(s). (Year). Associations of sleep and emotion regulation processes in ... [Article Title]. Retrieved from https://www.ncbi.nlm.nih.gov/pmc/articles/PMC9670771/

Cureus. (Year). Effects of Excessive Screen Time on Child Development. Retrieved from https://www.cureus.com/articles/162175-effects-of-excessive-screen-time-on-child-development-an-updated-review-and-strategies-for-management

American Academy of Pediatrics. (n.d.). Screen Time
Guidelines. Retrieved from
https://www.aap.org/en/patient-care/media-and-
children/center-of-excellence-on-social-media-
and-youth-mental-health/social-media-and-youth-
mental-health-q-and-a-portal/middle-
childhood/middle-childhood-questions/screen-
time-guidelines/

Psychology Today. (n.d.). A Research-Backed Guide to
Educational Apps for Children. Retrieved from
https://www.psychologytoday.com/us/blog/pare
nting-translator/202203/research-backed-guide-
educational-apps-children

StopBullying.gov. (n.d.). Prevent Cyberbullying.
Retrieved from
https://www.stopbullying.gov/cyberbullying/prev
ention

WebMD. (Year). Developmental Delays in Young
Children. Retrieved from
https://www.webmd.com/parenting/baby/recogn
izing-developmental-delays-birth-age-2

Parenting ADHD & Autism. (Year). ADHD in Kids: Top
5 Most Effective Parenting Strategies. Retrieved

from
https://parentingadhdandautism.com/2017/10/t
op-5-most-effective-parenting-strategies-for-kids-
with-adhd-hfa-asd/

The OT Hub. (n.d.). 8 Benefits of Individualised
Education Programs, for ... Retrieved from
https://www.theothub.com/article/8-benefits-of-
iep-for-students-with-learning-disabilities

Bright Horizons. (n.d.). Learning from Mistakes: Why
We Need to Let Children Fail. Retrieved from
https://www.brighthorizons.com/resources/Articl
e/the-importance-of-mistakes-helping-children-
learn-from-failure

Center on the Developing Child at Harvard University.
(n.d.). Resilience. Retrieved from
https://developingchild.harvard.edu/science/key-
concepts/resilience/

Meraki Lane. (n.d.). Critical Thinking: 11 Problem
Solving Activities for Kids. Retrieved from
https://www.merakilane.com/critical-thinking-
11-problem-solving-activities-for-kids/

KidCentral TN. (n.d.). Helping Children Through a
Difficult Time. Retrieved from
https://www.kidcentraltn.com/support/crisis-
services-for-children/helping-children-through-a-
difficult-time.html

Psychology Today. (Year). Why We Need to Teach
Kids Emotional Intelligence. Retrieved from
https://www.psychologytoday.com/us/blog/comp
assion-matters/201603/why-we-need-teach-k

ADOLESCENT Brain 101

Joyce T.

contents of this book and specifically disclaim any implied warranties of merchantability or fitness for a particular purpose. No warranty may be created or extended by sales representatives or written sales materials. The advice and strategies contained herein may not be suitable for your situation. You should consult with a professional when appropriate. Neither the publisher nor the author shall be liable for any loss of profit or any other commercial damages, including but not limited to special, incidental, consequential, personal, or other damages.

DEDICATION

To the parents and educators who show up, again and again, for our teenagers, even on the days when it feels like nothing you do is getting through: this is for you.

Through the stormy moods, the silences, the eye-rolls, the questions, and the unexpected joy, you stay present. You offer a listening ear, you give it your best, you love and you always keep learning and evolving. And even when it's hard (and let's be honest, it is hard), you don't give up.

To the parents who hold space for the messiness of growth, who anchor their teens with love while quietly weathering their own doubts—thank you. To the educators who go beyond lesson plans and venture into the teen mind and their well-being while still fostering academic success, may this dedication serve as a tribute to you.

With heartfelt gratitude for your ceaseless devotion,

Joyce T.

INTRODUCTION

"Adolescents are not monsters. They are just people trying to learn how to make it among the adults in the world, who are probably not so sure themselves."
- Virginia Satir

This quote by Virginia Satir, a well-known family therapist, offers a refreshingly kind and honest perspective on adolescence. It reminds us that teenagers, who often get labeled as difficult, dramatic, or rebellious, aren't really trying to cause trouble. They're only doing their best to figure out how to exist in a world built by adults, many of whom, let's face it, are still trying to figure things out too.

What Satir does so beautifully here is challenge the tired old stereotypes. She shifts the narrative from judgment to empathy. Teens aren't fundamentally different from adults; they're just earlier in the process. They're working through new emotions, responsibilities, and expectations, all while trying to make sense of who they are and where they belong.

The quote levels the playing field a bit because truthfully, none of us has everything figured out. We're all navigating some form of uncertainty. When we acknowledge this, we create room for understanding and connection instead of conflict. We stop seeing adolescence as a problem to fix and start seeing it as a very human part of the journey.

The transition from childhood to adulthood is anything but straightforward. It's a winding, often messy journey filled with big shifts – not just in the body, but in the brain too. During adolescence, the brain goes through a dramatic transformation, laying the groundwork for adult thinking, emotions, and behavior.

But let's be honest: the very changes that help teens grow up can also make them incredibly impulsive. They may feel like nothing can touch them—like they're invincible. If you've ever found yourself exasperated saying something along the lines of, *"What can you do, she's a teenager!"* then you understand how things can get. This phrase captures the tension so many adults feel: loving someone who's growing fast but not always thinking things through.

Thankfully, our understanding of what's actually going on in the adolescent brain has come a long way. Thanks to tools like MRI (magnetic resonance imaging), researchers can now safely and non-invasively look inside the living brain – something that used to be impossible without serious risks. We're now able to see how different parts of the brain grow, connect, and communicate during the teen years, and this has provided real insight into why adolescence feels the way it does, for teens *and* for the people around them.

Understanding what's happening inside the teen brain can offer more than just scientific insight, though; it can help us better connect with the young people in our lives. That's what this book is all about: *understanding the teenage brain so we can move from just surviving these years to truly understanding and thriving through them.*

I'm not here just to rattle off brain science, I'm here as a fellow parent. I've asked the same questions you have, felt the same frustration, and celebrated those small, hard-earned victories. Together, we'll explore the wild range of teenage emotions, the impact of technology and social media, the pressures of academics, body image, peer dynamics, impulsivity, and everything in between.

It might feel overwhelming at times, but don't worry – I'll be with you at every step, helping to translate the science into real-life understanding. If you're ready to understand the mysteries of the adolescent brain and transform your relationship with the teens in your life, then let's dive in together. Consider yourself officially welcomed!

THE TEEN BRAIN

What's Really Going On?

"We may not be able to prepare the future for our children, but we can at least prepare our children for the future."
~Franklin D. Roosevelt

Adolescence is one of those life stages we tend to forget just how strange it felt when we were in it. Somehow, once we've made it through, we look at today's teens as if they're unpredictable aliens, forgetting we once felt just as misunderstood, confused, and emotionally intense.

But here's the thing: the teenage brain isn't broken, and teens aren't being dramatic for fun. Their brains are in the middle of a major renovation. And while it might seem like this all wraps up by the end of the teen years, the truth is that development continues well into the mid-twenties.

This chapter is about understanding what's really going on in a teen's brain when they're riding emotional roller coasters, glued to their screens, lashing out, sleeping until noon, bursting with creativity, or throwing themselves into causes bigger than themselves.

The Prefrontal Cortex

Let's start with the prefrontal cortex. This part of the brain acts like the boss, which simply means it is responsible for decision-making, impulse control, emotional regulation, planning, and long-term thinking.

But during the teen years, it is still pretty new to the job. It's learning how to lead, how to pause before reacting, and how to weigh consequences before making a call. So when your teen blurts something out or makes a snap decision that seems obviously unwise, it's not because they aren't thinking. It's because their brain's prefrontal cortex is still in training.

You might find yourself asking, "What were they thinking?" The answer? They *were* thinking, just not with a fully developed prefrontal cortex.

The Amygdala

Next, there's the amygdala—a small, almond-shaped part of the brain that acts like an emotional alarm system. It processes feelings like fear, anxiety, and anger. During adolescence, the amygdala is on high alert. It's hypersensitive, constantly scanning for threats, real or imagined.

That's why something small can feel like a full-blown crisis. I remember one evening when my son tore through the house in near panic because his hoodie had gone missing. To me, it seemed like a minor hiccup. But for him, it was huge. That wasn't "teen drama," it was his amygdala sounding the alarm.

For teens, the emotional volume is turned way up, while their reasoning system (the prefrontal cortex) is still catching up. That imbalance explains a lot.

Neuroplasticity

Now for the good news: the teenage brain is incredibly adaptable. Thanks to neuroplasticity – our brain's ability to rewire and grow – it's primed to learn, change, and develop new skills faster than at almost any other time in life.

Think of neuroplasticity as the brain's construction crew. Every time your teen tries something new, like learning guitar, coding, or speaking up in class, their brain is laying down fresh neural pathways.

My younger son, for instance, picked up coding last year. At first, it felt completely foreign to him. But with time and practice, I could almost see his brain wiring new connections – his once-baffled look was slowly replaced by a cool and collected confidence.

Putting It All Together

So, in a nutshell, during the teenage years, your kids' brain boss (prefrontal cortex) is learning the ropes, their emotion alarm (amygdala) is super-sensitive, and their brain's superpower (neuroplasticity) is making them into learning superheroes.

Here's the bottom line: when your teenager does something that makes you scratch your head, just take a deep breath. It's not chaos; it's their brain at work. With your understanding and guidance, their brain will keep growing and getting better at this adulting thing. And hey, we're all in this together!

On Brain Development

Let's take a step back and look at how the brain grows, from those squishy baby beginnings all the way to early adulthood. Understanding the big picture helps us appreciate just how much is happening inside our kids' heads, and why certain behaviors at different stages make so much more sense when we look beneath the surface.

Early Childhood

In the early years, a child's brain undergoes processes that are truly remarkable. Think of a toddler learning to walk — those unsteady steps, the constant falling and trying again, and then suddenly, one day, they're off and running. While this may seem like just a physical milestone, it is also brain wiring in action.

This phase is called **synaptogenesis**, where the brain is rapidly forming new connections. It's like laying down roads between different neighborhoods in the brain – millions of them. And just like any overbuilt system, it eventually needs a clean-up. That's where **synaptic pruning** comes in.

Imagine a gardener trimming a tree, cutting back the weak or unused branches so the strongest ones can thrive. That's exactly what the brain does – it clears out what isn't being used to make room for stronger, faster, more efficient connections.

During this time, the brain is incredibly absorbent, like a super sponge. It soaks up everything – language, emotions, social cues, and routines. These early experiences become the blueprint for learning, behavior, and even long-term health. What a child is exposed to in these years *matters* more than we often realize.

Adolescence

Just when things feel like they've settled a bit, adolescence hits – and the brain launches into another huge phase of transformation. You could think of it as a second wave of construction, or like a massive software upgrade happening in real time.

Here, there's another round of synaptic pruning, this time focusing on higher-order thinking. The brain's efficiency is being fine-tuned, and **neuroplasticity** is at a high. This means teens are not only learning quickly, but also deeply affected by what they learn and experience during this stage.

But here's the catch: not all parts of the brain are developing at the same pace.

The amygdala, which handles emotions, fear, and rewards, matures earlier than the prefrontal cortex, the part responsible for impulse control, logic, and long-term planning. That's why teens can seem like walking contradictions – capable of deep insight one moment, and reckless decisions the next.

Add in the hormonal surges of puberty –testosterone, estrogen – and you've got what can feel like an emotional rollercoaster, complete with dramatic highs, confusing lows, and plenty of loop-the-loops.

Early Adulthood

As teens grow into young adults, the brain starts to stabilize. The prefrontal cortex finally catches up, and with that comes stronger decision-making, improved self-control, and more balanced emotional responses.

The brain's boss—who's been in training all this time—finally steps into the role with confidence.

At this stage, the brain begins to lose some of its neuroplasticity, meaning it's not quite as quick to rewire as it was during adolescence. But the tradeoff is more consistency, more clarity, and a stronger sense of self.

And here's something powerful to remember: the habits, skills, and emotional patterns built during the teen years don't just fade away. They lay the groundwork for adult life. That's why these years are so important, not just for survival, but for shaping the future.

Besides the brain, hormones play a massive role in teen behavior. Let's see how.

Hormones and Teenagers

The Impact of Testosterone

Testosterone often gets a bad rap, but it's far more complex than we give it credit for. It works behind the scenes, shaping our teens' moods, energy, and tempo without stepping into the spotlight.

In boys, especially, testosterone levels surge during adolescence, sparking obvious physical changes like a deeper voice or facial hair. But it also impacts the brain, influencing their behavior in subtle and not-so-subtle ways. It can increase competitiveness, intensify drive, and fuel the desire to push limits.

This might look like your teen suddenly throwing themselves into extreme sports, heated debates, or ambitious social causes.

But testosterone isn't just about risk – it also plays a role in social bonding. It encourages loyalty, close friendships, and that fierce urge to stand up for their tribe.

Estrogen

Estrogen takes center stage during puberty for girls, directing the development of physical changes like breast development and menstruation. But just like testosterone, behind the scenes, it's doing so much more.

Estrogen has a strong influence on mood and emotion, often turning adolescence into an emotional rollercoaster. It interacts with the brain's serotonin system — our natural mood stabilizer — and helps regulate learning, memory, and emotional resilience.

So if your typically calm daughter suddenly bursts into tears over something small or seems overwhelmed for no obvious reason, it's not melodrama, it's biology. Estrogen is amplifying emotions and sensitivity, sometimes making things feel much bigger than they seem on the outside.

Cortisol

Cortisol is the body's built-in alarm bell. When teens experience stress (and let's face it, there's plenty of that in adolescence), cortisol kicks in to help them stay alert and focused. In the short term, it's actually helpful — like a natural energy boost before a test or performance.

But if stress is constant, cortisol sticks around too long, and that can take a toll. Chronic stress can dull the brain's pleasure response, pushing teens to chase bigger thrills just to feel good, whether that's taking risks, staying out too late, or diving deep into social media rabbit holes.

So the next time your teen does something impulsive or seems unusually reactive, try to pause before labeling it as rebellion.

Case Study

Unlocking the Teenage Brain through Neuroscience

We've touched a little on neuroscience, and in this section, we'll explore real-life scenarios that will put this into context. These are moments that might feel familiar if you're raising or working with teens. We'll also look at how popular films and TV shows reflect these challenges, offering insight into what teens are feeling, not just how they act.

These stories bring science to life, helping us understand not only what's happening *in* the brain, but also *because* of it.

The Impact of Stress on Decision-Making

Declan's Exam Meltdown

Declan, a high school student and my son's friend, had spent days preparing for a big math test. He did everything right – studied hard, practiced problems, even got help from his teacher. But on the morning of the exam, things fell apart. He overslept, skipped breakfast, and rushed to school in a panic. Despite all his prep, Declan told my son that he struggled, blanked on answers, second-guessed himself, and left the test feeling frustrated and defeated.

What the Brain Tells Us

Declan's experience isn't about laziness or lack of effort – it's biology working against him. The stress of the situation triggered a spike in cortisol, the body's primary stress hormone. And while a little cortisol can sharpen focus, too much of it interferes with brain function, especially in the prefrontal cortex, the part of the brain responsible for reasoning, memory, and decision-making.

In teens, this part of the brain is still developing, making it even more vulnerable to stress. So in Declan's case, the pressure didn't just rattle him – it hijacked his ability to think clearly in the moment.

Pop Culture Parallel: Euphoria

In *Euphoria*, we see this theme through Rue's character, who struggles under academic and emotional pressure, often turning to self-destructive habits. The show highlights how stress and the adolescent brain's fragility are deeply intertwined and how high the stakes can feel for teens trying to hold it all together.

Hormonal Influence on Mood Swings

Cassie's Emotional Whiplash

When Cassie, my friend's daughter, was 15, she used to be easygoing and upbeat. But then suddenly, everything seemed to set her off. She would cry over small misunderstandings, have sudden irritability, and an emotional intensity that left her parents confused and, quite frankly, worried.

What the Brain Tells Us

Cassie's emotional shifts are tied to the hormonal changes going on inside her body, particularly the role of estrogen, which surges during puberty. Estrogen doesn't just drive physical changes; it also interacts with serotonin, a neurotransmitter that regulates mood. When these systems are in flux, emotions can swing wildly – sometimes within the same afternoon.

So while Cassie's reactions seemed out of proportion, they were not made-up or attention-seeking; they were real. Her brain and body were simply adjusting to a new hormonal landscape, and as of writing this book, she's still is learning how to manage what she's feeling.

Pop Culture Parallel: The Fault in Our Stars

Hazel Grace, the main character in *The Fault in Our Stars*, captures this emotional depth beautifully. Her experiences show us just how layered and powerful teen emotions can be, especially when hormones, identity, and life's big questions collide.

The Role of the Prefrontal Cortex in Risk-Taking Behavior

Mike and His High-Flying Hobbies

Mike, 17, is the daredevil of my son's friend group. He's always chasing the next adrenaline rush—BMX tricks, cliff diving, skateboarding off rooftops. His parents watch with a mix of awe and terror, wondering why he seems drawn to danger.

What the Brain Tells Us

Mike's thrill-seeking isn't just a personality trait; it's brain development at work. As we said, during adolescence, the prefrontal cortex (the region that helps assess risks and long-term consequences) is still under construction. Meanwhile, the brain's reward system is firing on all cylinders, encouraging excitement, novelty, and sensation.

This mismatch, high motivation, and low impulse control, is a big reason why teens are more likely to take risks. For Mike, the promise of fun outweighs the thought of injury.

Pop Culture Parallel: Every Teen Adventure Flick Ever

From *Stranger Things* to *The Hunger Games*, we see teens risking everything, often without hesitation. These stories resonate not because they're unrealistic, but because they tap into something very real: the teenage brain's deep craving for challenge, meaning, and intensity.

However, it's crucial to recognize that each teenager is unique. Their experiences, temperament, and environment contribute to shaping their behavior. While neuroscience provides a general framework, it doesn't offer a one-size-fits-all explanation. But it can help you replace judgment with compassion.

So the next time you witness an emotional meltdown or a risky leap (literally or metaphorically), take a breath. There's more going on than meets the eye, and at least now, you know what that "more" really is.

THE EMOTIONAL JOURNEY OF ADOLESCENCE

A Closer Look At Emotional Development

"Adolescence is a new birth, for the higher and more completely human traits are now born."

~G. Stanley Hall

In this chapter, we'll see how teenagers begin to make sense of their feelings, how those feelings shape their behavior, and what this emotional journey means for the adults walking beside them. Let's start with emotional maturity first:

Understanding Emotional Maturity

Emotional maturity is a bit like learning to steer your own ship through unpredictable waters, but if you're a teenager, that ship is still being built while you're already out at sea. It's confusing, exhilarating, and at times overwhelming.

As the teenage brain develops, so does the ability to recognize and manage emotions. It doesn't happen all at once. At first, they learn to name what they're feeling, whether it's anger, joy, anxiety, or embarrassment. Then, with time and experience, teens begin to understand where those feelings come from and how to respond in ways that are healthy rather than reactive.

It's kind of like learning an instrument. At the beginning, it's just about hitting the right notes. But with practice, rhythm and expression start to emerge. Eventually, it becomes music: real, emotional, deeply personal music.

You can see this kind of growth in literature, too. Take *Harry Potter*, for instance. At the start of the series, Harry is just a boy trying to make sense of a confusing world. But as the story progresses, we watch him wrestle with grief, loyalty, anger, love, and loss—learning to respond with courage and heart. His emotional growth doesn't come from having all the answers, but from being willing to face hard truths and grow through them, just like teens in the real world.

The Role of Empathy in Emotional Development

Empathy, the ability to feel what someone else is going through, is one of the most powerful tools in a teenager's emotional toolbox. But it doesn't come automatically. It takes practice.

When teens begin to develop empathy, their relationships deepen. Friendships become more meaningful, conflicts start to make more sense and even family dynamics can shift, as teens begin to see their parents and siblings not just as people in their way, but as people with their own emotions and struggles.

A beautiful example of empathy in literature is found in *To Kill a Mockingbird*. Through her father, Atticus, young Scout Finch learns to see the world through others' eyes, even when it's hard. She begins to understand that people's actions often come from pain or fear, and that empathy can lead to compassion. Like Scout, teens begin developing empathy not all at once, but through real-life experiences, small lessons, and self-reflection.

Emotional Intelligence in Teens

Emotional intelligence—or EQ—is like a GPS for navigating the emotional terrain of adolescence. It includes self-awareness (knowing what you feel), self-regulation (managing how you express it), motivation, empathy, and social skills. When teens begin to strengthen these emotional muscles, they're better able to handle stress, connect with others, and bounce back from setbacks.

Think of it as a toolkit. It doesn't guarantee life will be easy, but it gives teens the tools to face hard moments with more calm, confidence, and perspective.

One of the most honest portrayals of emotional intelligence can be found in *The Perks of Being a Wallflower*. Through his letters, Charlie opens up about his confusion, pain, and search for connection.

He doesn't always know what to do with his emotions, but he reflects on them with honesty and a hunger to understand. Over time, he learns how to sit with his feelings, talk about them, and reach out when he needs support. His journey is messy, but it's real. And it shows how powerful emotional intelligence can be, even when you're still figuring it all out.

The Powerful Role of Emotional Intelligence

When teens start to build emotional intelligence, they're not just preparing for high school or college; they're building a lifelong foundation. EQ helps them deal with disappointment, navigate conflict, find purpose, and build lasting relationships. And as adults, parents, teachers, and mentors, we play a key role in helping them develop these skills by modeling empathy, encouraging reflection, and staying present through the chaos.

A powerful example of emotional intelligence in context can be found in Frodo Baggins from *The Lord of the Rings*. Frodo's journey is filled with hardship, but what sets him apart isn't brute strength—it's his emotional strength. He shows resilience in the face of fear, compassion toward others in the fellowship, and an inner awareness that helps him resist the temptations of power. Frodo doesn't always get it right, but he leads with heart. And in many ways, that's what emotional intelligence is all about: not being perfect, but being human and choosing growth anyway.

How Do You Help Them Through Emotional Development?

Understanding aspects of emotional development in teenagers helps us guide them through this journey. As caretakers, we have the privilege of supporting them on this remarkable journey, offering guidance and understanding during these crucial years of emotional development.

Think about the classic coming-of-age novel *"The Catcher in the Rye"* by J.D. Salinger, where Holden Caulfield goes on a journey of self-discovery. Holden's caretakers, though not physically present, serve as guiding figures through his emotional turmoil. As readers, we witness the challenges of emotional development, the struggle to understand oneself, and the importance of supportive figures during this pivotal period.

This just goes to show you the essence of the role caretakers play in offering guidance and understanding during the crucial years of emotional development – and for your teen, you are the caretaker.

The Struggle of Emotional Regulation

Emotional Regulation Defined

Emotional regulation is quite a big concept, especially for teens. For them, it can feel a lot like trying to control the wind. Emotions come and go with such force and unpredictability, it's no wonder many of them feel overwhelmed by their inner world. But here's the hopeful part: like any skill, emotional regulation can be learned. With support, strategy, and practice, teens can begin to feel more in control of what they feel and how they respond.

In my own home, I've watched this unfold with my son, Mark. At first, managing emotions felt impossible for him. One moment he'd be calm, the next he'd be caught in a wave of frustration or sadness. But as we talked more openly about what was happening inside, and explored tools together, I began to see a shift. Emotional regulation wasn't some unreachable ideal—it was a muscle he could strengthen, one step at a time.

Identifying Emotional Triggers

We all have emotional triggers, those little buttons that, when pushed, set off big reactions. For teens, these can range from offhand comments about their appearance to the heavy weight of academic pressure. The first step in managing emotions is learning to recognize what sets them off.

With Mark, it became clear that school stress was one of his biggest triggers. We started noticing patterns: irritability before exams, withdrawal after tough assignments. I encouraged him to keep a simple feelings journal, just to write down what he was feeling and what happened right before. That tiny habit made a big difference. It helped both of us connect the dots, and it gave him a way to name what he was experiencing instead of just reacting to it.

This kind of self-awareness is the foundation of emotional regulation. When teens can anticipate what might set them off, they're far better equipped to manage how they respond.

The Role of Mindfulness

Mindfulness is a word that gets thrown around a lot these days, but at its core, it's really about being present, fully aware of what's happening in the moment without judgment. For teens, who often feel pulled in a million directions emotionally, mindfulness can be a lifeline.

We started with simple things. For Mark, just taking a few deep breaths before reacting to something stressful made a difference. It was like switching on a flashlight in a dark room. He began to notice his feelings more clearly before they took over, and over time, he started responding more thoughtfully.

Mindfulness doesn't have to be complicated. It can be a short breathing exercise, a walk where you focus on what you see and hear, or even just checking in with how your body feels. The goal isn't to eliminate feelings—it's to get curious about them instead of being ruled by them.

Guided Imagery

One of our favorite tools has been guided imagery. When things feel too intense or overwhelming, I'll gently ask Mark to close his eyes and picture a place that feels safe and calming, whether that's a forest, a beach, or even a cozy spot in our home. He takes a few minutes to imagine it in full detail: the sounds, the smells, the textures. It becomes his mental "reset button."

In those moments, it's like giving his brain a short vacation—a break from the noise and pressure. We also paired this with Progressive Muscle Relaxation, or PMR, another simple but powerful way to release built-up tension in the body.

Progressive Muscle Relaxation (PMR)

Stress often shows up in our bodies before we even realize what's wrong, for instance, tight shoulders, clenched jaws, or fidgety limbs. PMR helps teens tune into those physical signs of stress and learn how to let them go.

It works like this: you ask your teen to slowly tense and then relax each muscle group, starting from the feet and working their way up. With practice, it becomes almost automatic—a way to recognize when the body is holding stress and gently invite it to release.

Mark was skeptical at first (most teens are), but after a few sessions, he started requesting it on his own. It's now one of his go-to tools when he's feeling overwhelmed.

Keep in mind that no one masters emotional regulation overnight, least of all teens, whose brains and bodies are still learning how to handle the intensity of this life stage. But with patience, trust, and a few simple strategies, they can build the skills they need to ride out the emotional waves with more balance and confidence.

Managing Emotional Outbursts

Let's be honest, when it comes to teens, emotional outbursts are a consistent part of the ride. While they can be exhausting, they're also incredibly normal.

The key is not to fear the outbursts, but to help teens learn what to do afterward. Self-calming techniques like deep breathing can work wonders in the moment. When teens learn to slow their breath, they're actually turning off their brain's "fight-or-flight" switch, helping themselves calm down from the inside out.

With Mark, deep breathing became our go-to. In the early days, I'd remind him gently to pause and breathe. Now, he often catches himself and starts doing it without prompting. After the storm passes, we talk. We dig into what really caused the outburst: Was it frustration? Embarrassment? Pressure? That reflection has become a powerful part of his growth, turning difficult moments into learning ones.

Being a Role Model

It's easy to forget that our kids don't just listen to what we say, they watch what we do. When it comes to handling emotions, we are their blueprint.

I've made it a personal goal to be more intentional with how I express my own feelings. If I'm overwhelmed, I say it. If I need a moment, I take it. And when I mess up? I apologize. This models what healthy emotional regulation looks like.

Mark's picked up more than I realized. One day, after a rough evening, he said, "I need a minute to cool down—like you do." That's when I knew that our reactions as parents are indeed influential.

But remember, teaching emotional regulation isn't about never feeling upset. It's about showing our kids how to ride the wave without getting swept away.

Navigating the Emotional Sea

We've used the sea metaphor when it comes to teen emotions, so let's carry it along here as well. With adolescence, some days are calm, others stormy, and most have waves that come out of nowhere. Teens are learning basically how to sail, and our job, as parents or educators, is to be the compass they can turn to when the waters get rough.

We don't have to control the weather for them, but we can offer guidance, tools, and reassurance that they're not alone out there.

In our home, this metaphor has become part of our language. When Mark feels overwhelmed, I might say, "Looks like the waves are high today. Want help steering?" That simple shift—from reacting to guiding—has helped us both stay connected in the hard moments.

With time and practice, teens start to navigate their own emotions with more confidence. They become stronger, more self-aware, and more capable of sailing through whatever life throws at them.

The Impact of Stress on Teen Emotions

The Physiological Response to Stress

Imagine starting your morning with a sudden loud alarm, your heart races, your palms sweat, and you instantly feel alert. That's your body's stress response, and teens experience it all the time, not just in emergencies, but in everyday situations like tough tests, social pressure, or conflict with friends.

Their bodies release hormones like adrenaline and cortisol, preparing them to "fight or flee." But because their brains are still developing, that rush of stress can feel especially intense, and it can easily tip into frustration, anxiety, or even anger.

The Link Between Stress and Anxiety

Stress and anxiety are closely connected cousins. Stress often comes from a clear source, a deadline, a performance, or a confrontation. But anxiety can sneak up on you and stick around long after the stressor is gone. It's like the brain stays on high alert, even when there's no immediate danger.

When teens face chronic stress, their brains can get wired to expect the worst. For instance, a math test they did a while back that didn't go too well might trigger worry on a relaxing weekend. Their nervous system keeps ringing the alarm bell, even when the coast is clear.

I've seen this happen with Mark, especially around school. Even when things were going well, he'd feel unsettled—like something was about to go wrong. That's anxiety creeping in, whispering fear where calm should be.

Chronic Stress and Anxiety

Stress, in moderation, isn't all bad. It can motivate teens to study, perform, and grow. But when stress lingers—when it becomes a constant background hum—it can drain energy, disrupt sleep, and affect both physical and mental health.

That's why teaching teens how to *work with* stress is more important than trying to eliminate it. We can't protect them from every challenge, but we can give them tools to manage those challenges more effectively.

Start by helping them name what stress feels like in their bodies. Do they get headaches? Feel tense? Lose focus? That kind of awareness is the first step in self-regulation.

Navigating the Sea of Stress

Stress can feel overwhelming, but with the right tools—and the right support—teens can learn to ride those waves, even appreciate them as part of their growth.

Our role isn't to remove all stress, but to help teens become resilient. That means teaching them to breathe, to reflect, to rest when they need it, and to reach out when it gets too much.

In our family, we talk about stress the same way we talk about the weather. Some days are stormy. Some are bright. But every day is navigable with the right map and mindset.

Let's keep helping them cope and reminding them that we're right there, sailing beside them.

Case Studies

Handling Emotional Outbursts Explained

In this section, we will cover several real-life examples and what to do, just in case you find yourself in similar situations:

Scenario 1: Dealing with Academic Pressure

Explanation:

Laura's emotional outbursts are triggered by the stress of upcoming finals. In this scenario, providing support involves a multifaceted approach:

Validating Emotions:

Why: Emotional validation helps Laura feel understood and acknowledged.

How: Encouraging her to express her feelings and reassuring her that stress is a normal response to academic challenges.

Study Strategies:

Why: Breaking down tasks reduces anxiety and makes studying more manageable.

How: Assisting Laura in creating a study schedule, allowing her to focus on one task at a time, promoting a sense of control.

Prioritize Self-Care:

Why: Self-care enhances mood and cognitive function, crucial during stressful times.

How: Reminding Laura to maintain regular meals, engage in physical activity, and get adequate sleep.

Perspective on Grades:

Why: Reinforcing that worth is not solely defined by grades promotes a healthier mindset.

How: Offering reassurance, highlighting strengths, and acknowledging achievements outside academics.

Scenario 2: Managing Family Conflict

Explanation:

Lily's emotional outbursts stem from frequent conflicts with her parents. Addressing this situation involves building healthy communication and conflict resolution skills:

Open Communication:

Why: Creating an open and respectful family environment fosters understanding.

How: Encouraging active listening and providing a platform for family members to express feelings and perspectives.

Expressing Feelings:

Why: Teaching Lily to express feelings calmly reduces confrontations.

How: Introducing the use of "I" statements to communicate personal feelings without blaming or criticizing.

Empathy:

Why: Empathy promotes understanding, reducing conflict.

How: Emphasizing the importance of seeing situations from different perspectives, cultivating a more empathetic family dynamic.

Emotional outbursts during adolescence are a common aspect of emotional development. The most important thing is to understand the causes behind such outbursts, acknowledge emotions, and equip teenagers with strategies to express feelings healthily.

THE 3 FACTORS

The Persistent Triad in Teen Development

"Even as kids reach adolescence, they need more than ever for us to watch over them. Adolescence is not about letting go. It's about hanging on during a very bumpy ride."

~Ron Taffel

There always seem to be a few pieces of the puzzle that show up again and again when it comes to teens, and they're not always easy to figure out. But if you look closely, three key factors stand out as powerful forces that shape nearly every teen's experience.

In this chapter, we'll take a look at those three core influences, beginning with one that's often underestimated but deeply important: sleep.

The Late-Night Mystery Explained

Changes in Sleep Cycle

Teens are notorious night owls – we all know it. But what's really going on under the surface? Is it that they force themselves awake, or are there biological factors at play that keep them awake?

Sleep Phase Delay

The body's internal clock, known as the circadian rhythm, experiences a shift called sleep phase delay during adolescence. This leads to increased alertness later in the evening, making early bedtimes challenging. This biological shift helps you understand why teens may naturally struggle with early bedtimes.

Morning Wake-Up

The natural tendency for teens to wake up later is a result of their set internal clock. Recognizing this biological aspect can help you to reframe possible perceptions of your teen(s) being lazy and emphasize the importance of aligning schedules with their natural sleep patterns.

Impact on Health and Academics

Health Effects

Poor sleep during adolescence can affect mood, energy levels, and physical health, which adds stress to the already existing emotional rollercoaster of adolescence. This highlights the interconnectedness of sleep and overall well-being during a crucial developmental period.

Academic Performance

You've probably seen it: your teen staying up late to cram for a test, hoping those last-minute study hours will give them an edge. But here's the truth, without enough sleep, the brain struggles to absorb, process, and hold on to new information. Those late-night efforts might actually backfire. Helping teens connect the dots between sleep and academic success reinforces the message that rest isn't a luxury; it's part of the plan.

Tips for Healthy Sleep Habits

<u>Consistent Schedule</u>

Encourage a consistent sleep schedule, even on weekends. This is recommended to help your teen align with the internal clock. Consistency is a key factor in making sure this is possible.

Bedroom Environment

The bedroom should be a place of calm. Encourage teens to create a quiet, cozy environment that supports good sleep. Things like blackout curtains, earplugs, or a soft white noise machine can help. Even little changes in lighting or temperature can make a big difference.

Limit Screen Time

Phones, tablets, and TVs give off blue light that messes with melatonin, the hormone that helps us sleep. Powering down screens at least an hour before bed can help teens wind down naturally. This might be the hardest habit to change, but it's also one of the most effective.

Get Moving

Daily exercise, especially in the morning or early afternoon, helps teens sleep better at night. Physical activity boosts the body's natural rhythms and can reduce anxiety and restlessness, two major sleep disruptors.

Wind Down Routine

Bedtime routines aren't just for toddlers. Teens benefit from relaxing rituals too, whether it's reading a book, taking a warm shower, or doing a few minutes of mindful breathing. These small habits signal the brain that it's time to shift from busy mode to rest mode.

Now, let's move on to the second factor:

Rebellion

The Rebellious Stage as a Quest for Independence

In homes worldwide, the familiar scene of a defiant teenager breaking rules plays out. However, beyond this stubbornness lies the deep need for autonomy and independence, which, if we may resist, we may view as rebellion.

Let's understand this in detail:

Drive for Autonomy

- Powerful Urge: The teenage drive for autonomy is a deep-seated urge to control their lives, not mere rebellion.

- Becoming Independent: Teens want to make choices, learn from mistakes, and carve their own path. It's a healthy step toward independence.

Role of Peer Influence

- Peer Power: Peers wield influence during adolescence, both positive and negative, amplifying the drive for independence.

- Positive Influence: Peers can inspire positive independence, encouraging teens to explore, try new activities, and find a sense of belonging.

Ways to Support Healthy Independence

- Negotiate Boundaries: Involve your teens in setting boundaries through discussion, fostering autonomy, and teaching negotiation skills.

- Encourage Decision-Making: Provide opportunities for them to make decisions, which can boost their confidence and refine decision-making skills.

- Respect Privacy: Respect their need for physical and emotional privacy to build trust and reinforce autonomy.

- Support Interests: Encourage them to explore their interests and hobbies, providing avenues for self-expression and independence.

- Guide, Don't Control: Remember to focus on guiding rather than controlling. Share wisdom, provide advice, and let them make decisions, fostering autonomy while assuring support.

Real-Life Scenario

Susan and Ben

Susan was a single mother to her son Ben and their home had started to feel like a battleground. Ben was pushing back on rules, staying out late, and constantly questioning everything Susan asked of him. At first, it felt like rebellion, like he was deliberately testing her boundaries just to make life harder.

But over time, Susan began to shift her approach. Instead of reacting with frustration, she started to really listen. She realized that Ben's behavior wasn't about disrespect, it was his way of asserting independence, of saying, "I need to figure out who I am."

Through open conversations, Susan made space for Ben to express himself. They talked about why certain rules mattered and where there could be room for flexibility. As time went by, it became clear that Ben wasn't trying to push her away; he was trying to find his own footing in the world.

Rebellion, as it turns out, is often less about defying authority and more about discovering identity. When we approach it with patience, curiosity, and respect, it becomes a chance to strengthen, not sever, the connection with our teens.

Now, on to the third factor:

The Social Aspect

Teens and Their Tribal Tendencies

As kids move into adolescence, peers often take center stage where they once looked to parents for approval. This is a natural, necessary part of growing up. Teens are wired to seek connection outside the home as they begin carving out their own identity.

In this section, we will see why peer relationships matter so much during this stage, how social dynamics shape behavior, and what we can do to support teens as they navigate their "tribe."

Importance of Peer Relationships

Shift in Spotlight

- Explanation: Adolescence redirects attention from family to friends, emphasizing the increasing influence of peer opinions.
- Relevance: Recognizing this shift helps parents and caregivers understand the evolving dynamics in teens' lives.

Emotional Support

- Explanation: Peer relationships serve as a safe space for teens to share emotions, fostering a sense of belonging and understanding.
- Relevance: Highlighting the emotional support aspect underscores the importance of these relationships in teens' lives.

Role of Social Acceptance

Guiding Rhythm

- Explanation: Acceptance by peers is portrayed as the guiding rhythm in teenage social life, aligning with the human need for social connection.

- Relevance: Understanding the importance of social acceptance helps caregivers navigate and support teens in their social interactions.

Validation and Self-Esteem

- Explanation: Social acceptance is linked to the validation of teens' self-worth, contributing to boosted self-esteem and reinforced identity.

- Relevance: Connecting social acceptance to self-esteem highlights its profound impact on teens' mental and emotional well-being.

Conformity Pressures

- Explanation: The pursuit of acceptance can lead to conformity, influencing attitudes, behaviors, and choices to fit in.

- Relevance: Acknowledging conformity pressures raises awareness of the challenges teens may face in balancing their individuality with the desire for acceptance.

In the next chapter, we turn our attention to something often felt but not always seen — the emotional and mental health struggles that many teens quietly carry. Behind the eye rolls, mood swings, or silence at dinner, there can be deeper challenges like anxiety, stress, or even depression.

Let's understand this better.

THE TEEN BRAIN AND MENTAL HEALTH

Unmasking the Invisible Battles

"We live in a world where mental health is real. Emotional health is real, and people feel like no one cares."

- Malik Yoba

We've spent some time exploring the teen brain, how it develops, what influences it, and how emotions and peer dynamics come into play. But now, we're zooming in on something just as critical, yet often hidden beneath the surface: mental health.

Let's be honest, teenage life is a lot. Between navigating friendships, growing independence, academic stress, and figuring out who they are, teens are often juggling more than we realize. On the outside, everything might seem fine, like that laid-back kid at a party who looks totally chill. But underneath, there might be a mental and emotional tug-of-war going on.

At the core of it is the developing teen brain. While we've already explored how the prefrontal cortex is still maturing and the limbic system often takes the lead, here's where it becomes more than just a quirky phase. This mismatch between emotional highs and a still-learning logic system can make teens more vulnerable to anxiety, depression, and emotional overwhelm. And often, those feelings aren't voiced – they're masked.

This chapter is about unmasking it all. It's about understanding how mental health challenges show up during adolescence—not always loudly, but deeply. We'll explore what's really going on inside, why some teens are more vulnerable than others, and how we as parents, caregivers, and educators can spot the signs and offer meaningful support.

Indeed, there's no magic fix, but there is power in empathy, awareness, and early action. As we dig deeper, we will not only learn about the adolescent mind but also how to walk beside our teens with compassion and an understanding presence, which is what they need from us.

We will do this through quick descriptions that you can easily understand.

Let's go!

Navigating Anxiety and Stress in the Teen Maze

Recognizing Signs of Anxiety

- Description: Anxiety is a master of disguise, wearing different masks such as restlessness, physical discomfort, and avoidance behaviors.
- Example: Your teenager might steer clear of social situations, express physical symptoms like a racing heart, or undergo changes in sleep and eating patterns.

Impact on Daily Life

- Description: Anxiety acts as a lens distorting a teenager's view of the world, affecting various aspects of their daily life, including school, social interactions, hobbies, and family time.

- Example: Within the classroom, anxiety may create challenges in concentration and active participation, turning routine tasks into daunting sources of stress.

Strategies for Stress Management

Open Conversations:

- Description: Create a safe and non-judgmental space for your teenager to openly express fears and worries.
- Example: Employ empathetic responses such as *"That sounds really tough"* to foster an environment conducive to open dialogue.

Breathing Exercises

- Description: Introduce simple yet effective techniques like deep breathing to help calm the nervous system.
- Example: Encourage the regular practice of these exercises as a proactive measure whenever anxiety starts to surface.

Mindfulness Practices

- Description: Incorporate mindfulness practices, such as meditation or yoga, to keep teens grounded in the present moment.
- Example: Suggest the integration of mindfulness techniques into their daily routine as a tool for managing stress.

Encourage Physical Activity

- Description: Promote regular physical exercise as a healthy outlet for anxiety, leveraging the mood-boosting effects of endorphins.
- Example: Encourage participation in sports, dance, or other fitness activities as part of their routine.

Balanced Diet and Sleep

- Description: Emphasize the crucial role of nutrition and adequate sleep in regulating mood and stress levels.
- Example: Discuss the connection between a well-balanced diet, quality sleep, and overall emotional well-being.

Seek Professional Help

- Description: Recognize the severity of anxiety when it significantly interferes with daily life and advocate for the involvement of mental health professionals.

- Example: Take proactive steps to connect your teenager with a supportive therapist or counselor who specializes in adolescent mental health.

Depression in Teens

Recognizing Signs of Teen Depression

Teen depression often sneaks in quietly, disguising itself as typical teenage behavior. For instance, Jane, a close friend's daughter, started becoming more irritable, reacting strongly to minor annoyances. She withdrew into solitude, spending long hours alone in her room. Jane's parents noticed that the activities she once enjoyed, like playing the guitar or painting, lost their luster, replaced by a pervasive indifference.

As depression took hold of Jane, her academic performance started to falter. Her once-enthusiastic participation in school clubs and sports became an afterthought, and meals went untouched. Constant fatigue plagued her, like a car running on empty.

Also, Jane's sleep patterns shifted, with nights spent staring at the ceiling and days lost to excessive sleep.

The Crucial Role of Support and Understanding

In the face of teen depression, your role as a parent or educator becomes crucial. If you notice signs of depression in your teen, approach them with kindness and empathy. For instance, Tom, a neighbor's son. Tom's parents initiated a conversation, not a confrontation. They let him know they had noticed his struggle and that they were there to help, free from judgment or criticism.

Tom's parents utilized active listening techniques to convey genuine interest. They allowed him to express his feelings, fears, and struggles without interruption or the pressure of quick fixes. Their mere presence and understanding proved immensely helpful to Tom. Even if you can't fully grasp their experience, acknowledge their pain and validate their feelings.

For example, when Tom expressed feelings of worthlessness or guilt, his parents reassured him that it's okay to feel the way he does and reminded him that he's not alone. They communicated that depression is treatable, and with the right help, he can overcome it.

The Importance of Professional Help

While your support is invaluable, professional help often becomes necessary in dealing with teen depression. Take Jess, a family friend's daughter, for instance. A mental health professional provided a safe space for her to explore her feelings and equipped her with effective coping strategies.

Psychotherapy, especially cognitive-behavioral therapy (CBT) and interpersonal therapy (IPT), proved effective in treating Jess's teen depression. In some cases, medication was recommended, helping to balance brain chemicals and alleviate symptoms. Jess's parents emphasized that seeking professional help is not a sign of weakness but a step towards healing.

They reminded her that taking care of mental health is as important as physical health. Jess, like many others, needed to be reassured that she is not alone, help is available, and things can get better.

Navigating the Storm towards Hope and Healing

Depression can feel like a heavy storm cloud settling over what should be a bright, spirited season of life. For many teenagers, it quietly creeps in, sometimes showing up as sadness, sometimes as anger, withdrawal, or simply exhaustion. And for the adults who love them, it can be confusing and painful to witness.

But here's the hopeful part: depression is not the end of the road. With compassion, understanding, and the right support—whether through family, school, therapy, or all of the above—healing is not only possible, it's within reach.

Understanding Academic Stress and the Teen Brain

The Shadow of Academic Stress

In the middle of the highs and lows of adolescence, one factor stands tall like a towering skyscraper: academic stress. It rises above everything with school deadlines, tough exams, never-ending homework, college applications, and the unspoken pressure to always do more, be more, achieve more.

This pressure doesn't come from one place. It builds slowly, from expectations at home, comparisons with peers, the pursuit of perfection, and sometimes, from teens' own inner critics. The message they receive again and again is clear: their worth is tied to their grades, their test scores, and their accomplishments. But where does that leave space for their creativity, their kindness, their joy?

The Balancing Act

It's true that a little pressure can be motivating. It can spark ambition and help teens discover what they're capable of. But when that pressure becomes constant, when the fear of failure overshadows the love of learning, it turns something potentially positive into a chronic source of stress. Suddenly, the drive to do well becomes a burden teens carry every day.

The Complex Relationship with Mental Health

Academic stress doesn't exist in a vacuum. It's deeply ingrained into a teenager's life and emotions, test by test, grade by grade. When the pressure starts to build, it doesn't just affect how they perform in school; it affects how they see themselves.

Over time, constant stress can wear down even the most resilient teen. It can quietly open the door to anxiety, self-doubt, or depression. And because the teenage brain is still developing—particularly the areas that regulate emotion—teens often don't yet have the tools to manage that pressure in a healthy way.

What's more, when academic achievement becomes the measuring stick for worth, a single low grade can feel like a personal failure. Instead of seeing it as just a rough day or a tough subject, they may internalize it: *"I'm not smart enough," "I'll never catch up,"* or even, *"I'm a disappointment."* Their self-esteem starts to ride the highs and lows of their report cards, turning school into something that brings them great stress.

Strategies for a Balanced Academic Life

Think of academic pressure like steam building in a pressure cooker; it can be useful in small amounts, but if there's no way to release it, things can explode. That's why it's so important to help teens find their own "release valves," small, sustainable ways to manage stress before it becomes overwhelming:

Prioritize and Plan

Teach your teen to prioritize tasks based on urgency and importance. Using planners or digital tools to organize tasks and deadlines can help manage workload effectively and reduce stress.

Break it Down

Encourage your teen to break large tasks or projects into smaller, manageable parts. This approach makes the overall task seem less overwhelming and more achievable.

Healthy Study Habits

Promote healthy study habits, including regular breaks, studying in a quiet environment, and avoiding last-minute cramming. Effective study techniques like active recall and spaced repetition can enhance learning.

Self-Care

Remind your teen of the importance of self-care, encompassing regular exercise, a balanced diet, and adequate sleep. These practices can boost mood, energy levels, and cognitive function, contributing to effective stress management.

Open Communication

Maintain open lines of communication with your teen. Let them know they can share academic concerns without fear of judgment or criticism. Validate their feelings and stressors, reassuring them of your unconditional support.

In the face of academic stress, it's crucial to remind teenagers that their academic achievements do not define their worth. They are more than a score on a test or a grade on a report card; they are individuals bursting with potential, each possessing unique strengths, passions, and dreams.

Nurturing Resilience and Individuality

As parents and educators, our role is to help navigate academic stress, providing the tools needed to create a balanced academic life. We support, understand, and stand by our teenagers, showing them they are not alone in their struggles. We emphasize the importance of mental health and celebrate their individuality, valuing who they are over what they achieve on a test.

In the next part of this chapter, we'll take a closer look at something every teenager needs in their emotional toolkit: resilience. It's one of the most important qualities we can help them build. We'll explore what resilience really means, why it matters so much in adolescence, and how the relationships in a teen's life—especially with family, teachers, and friends—play a powerful role in shaping it.

Crafting Emotional Armor for Teens

The Power of Resilience

If there's one quality that carries teens through the ups and downs of growing up, it's resilience. Think of it like a strong, flexible sailboat—able to stay afloat and steer even when the winds shift and the waves get rough. It doesn't mean the storm won't come. It just means your teen has what it takes to make it through—and even come out stronger.

Resilience isn't about avoiding problems or always staying calm under pressure. It's about learning how to recover when things go wrong, how to keep going even when the path isn't clear, and how to believe in yourself even when you're shaken. When stress, anxiety, or setbacks show up (as they often do), resilience gives teens the confidence to keep moving forward—to ask for help when they need it, to face fears with courage, and to know deep down: "I can get through this."

The Crucial Role of Positive Relationships

Resilience is a connection that is nurtured – with parents, siblings, teachers, friends, and mentors. These relationships form the scaffolding that supports teens as they learn to weather life's challenges.

- **Parents**

Your steady presence is more powerful than you might think. When your teen knows you're there no matter what, with love that doesn't waver and support that doesn't depend on performance, they feel grounded. That deep sense of being seen and accepted gives them the confidence to face hard things and the self-worth to bounce back after failure.

- **Teachers**

A kind, supportive teacher can make all the difference. In a safe, inclusive classroom where students are encouraged to try, fail, and try again, teens begin to see mistakes not as dead ends but as part of the process. When teachers believe in them—even on the days they struggle—it plants the seed of resilience.

- **Friends and Mentors**

Peers and trusted adults outside the family also play a big role. In the messiness of adolescence, having someone to laugh with, vent to, or share life's weird little moments with helps teens feel understood and less alone. Through these shared experiences, they learn about mutual support, empathy, and standing by others through thick and thin.

Strategies for Building Resilience

Here are some thoughtful, practical ways to support your teen in developing the emotional grit they need for the road ahead:

Promote Problem-Solving Skills

When your teen is facing a tough situation, resist the urge to jump in with the answer. Instead, sit beside them and work through it together. Help them see the issue not as an impossible wall but as a puzzle that can be figured out step by step. Brainstorm ideas, weigh the pros and cons of each option, and guide them toward choosing their own path forward. You're not just solving one problem—you're teaching them how to face many.

Foster a Growth Mindset

Cultivate a growth mindset in your teen. Teach them that abilities and intelligence can be developed with effort and persistence. Emphasize the value of hard work, perseverance, and grit in achieving their goals.

Encourage Self-Expression

Provide ample opportunities for your teen to express their feelings, thoughts, and ideas. Whether through conversations, journal writing, or creative activities like art and music, self-expression boosts self-esteem and fosters a sense of control, both crucial for resilience.

Nurture Optimism

Life won't always be easy, but helping your teen learn to spot the silver lining can make a world of difference. Talk with them about challenges as temporary rather than permanent. Encourage them to notice what went right, even in hard situations. By no means is optimism about denying pain; it's about believing there's still a way forward.

Validate Feelings

Validate your teen's feelings. Acknowledge their emotions without judgment or criticism. Let them know it's okay to feel upset, scared, or sad, as validation enhances emotional awareness and regulation.

As parents and educators, resilience is one of the greatest gifts we can give our teens. Every moment we spend guiding them, listening to them, and walking beside them through setbacks is like adding another plank to the ship they'll eventually sail on their own. And with every storm they weather, they grow sturdier, braver, and more sure of who they are.

Next, we'll turn our focus to another major force shaping the teen experience today: **technology and social media**. How is it affecting their attention, self-image, and mental health? How do we help them find balance in a world that never turns off? Let's see this together in the next chapter.

THE DIGITAL DILEMMA

Navigating the Impact of Technology on the Adolescent Brain

"As the world becomes a more digital place, we cannot forget about the human connection".
-Adam Neumann

We're raising kids in a world that's changing at lightning speed, especially when it comes to technology. From smartphones to social media, today's teens are growing up with digital tools that we, as adults, never had to navigate during our own adolescence. And while there's no doubt that these tools have transformed how we communicate, connect, and learn, they're also shaping something far more intimate and delicate: the teenage brain.

A recent study published in *JAMA Pediatrics* shed new light on this digital-age phenomenon. The findings suggest that frequent social media use may be doing more than keeping teens glued to their phones—it could actually be influencing the way their brains develop. Specifically, the study found that habitual use appears to activate brain regions linked to **social rewards and punishments**, nudging young brains to become more sensitive to peer feedback.

What's Really Going On in the Brain?

Researchers observed that adolescents who regularly check social media show changes in areas of the brain tied to emotion and decision-making, especially the amygdala (as we saw, our emotional radar) and the dorsolateral prefrontal cortex (the part responsible for reasoning and judgment). These regions seem to be tuning themselves to seek social rewards, likes, comments, views, and avoid perceived social rejection.

It's important to pause here: this doesn't necessarily mean that social media is harming their brains. But it does point to an important shift. These teens may be developing heightened sensitivity to social cues, both online and off, which could shape how they engage with the world around them.

Because adolescence is such a crucial time for brain development, the big question is: What does this mean long-term? That's still unclear. The science is still catching up. But what we do know is this: the brain is adaptable. Thanks to the concept of neuroplasticity, which we covered earlier, the brain can rewire itself based on experiences, meaning these changes are not necessarily permanent.

Screen Time and Childhood Development

And it's not just teens. This research adds to a broader conversation about screen time and its effects on younger children, especially during early development. For instance, excessive screen exposure in toddlers has been linked to language delays and attention challenges.

Then came the pandemic—a time when screens became lifelines for school, socializing, and sanity.

But the dramatic increase in screen time during this period created new complexities. Virtual learning, Zoom fatigue, isolation from peers, etc., these experiences have left lasting imprints, and we're still working to fully understand them.

Your Role as a Parent

One thing we do know is that parents play a crucial role in helping teens navigate their digital world. And since the prefrontal cortex is still under construction until around age 21, teenagers often need someone to step in as a kind of temporary stand-in.

Think of yourself as a "surrogate frontal lobe." You're there to help them pause, reflect, weigh consequences, and learn how to make better decisions online and offline.

This doesn't mean taking control or banning all screen time. It means creating open, ongoing conversations about what they're seeing, feeling, and experiencing online. It means talking about both the good and the bad—how social media can connect us but also leave us feeling left out or judged.

It's easy to slip into an all-or-nothing mindset when it comes to tech, either it's ruining our kids, or it's the greatest innovation ever. But the truth is somewhere in between. Social media and screen time can be both empowering and overwhelming. Teens can use digital platforms to explore their passions, connect with others, and find their voice. But they also need guidance to recognize when their use becomes excessive or starts to impact their well-being.

That's where you come in—as the steady, compassionate voice reminding them of their worth beyond likes and shares, and helping them find balance in a digital world that never really powers down.

In this chapter, we'll explore the delicate relationship between technology—particularly social media—and the adolescent brain. As our world becomes increasingly digital, screens have become a central part of daily life, especially for teens. Social media, in particular, plays a powerful role in how they communicate, connect, and view themselves.

We'll dive into what current research is revealing about how frequent use of social media might be influencing brain development, especially in areas linked to emotions, judgment, and sensitivity to social feedback. While some of these findings raise important questions, they also offer insight into how adaptable and responsive the teenage brain truly is.

Let's get started:

Navigating the Digital Landscape

In this constantly buzzing digital world, teens often find themselves doing five things at once: texting a friend, scrolling through Instagram, watching YouTube, flipping between homework tabs, and maybe even listening to music in the background. It feels like multitasking, and on the surface, it might even seem productive.

But here's the truth: the brain doesn't work that way. Research tells us that this kind of multitasking actually drains mental resources. It's like trying to listen to three different radio stations at the same time—you don't really catch the full message from any of them. Instead of saving time, multitasking often leads to more mistakes, lower productivity, and mental fatigue.

And the impact doesn't stop there. All that screen time—especially at night—can wreak havoc on sleep. The blue light from devices messes with melatonin, the hormone that helps us fall asleep. Think of it like having a digital espresso shot right before bed. Add in how engaging and addictive digital content can be, and suddenly it's midnight before your teen even notices the time. Over time, this lack of rest chips away at mood, focus, and overall well-being.

So, how do we help our teens navigate this fast-paced digital terrain without completely cutting them off from the world they live in?

To do this, here are some guidelines:

Set Clear Boundaries

Establish a family media plan with clear boundaries for screen time. Rules such as no screens during meals or a digital curfew an hour before bed can be effective. It's crucial to lead by example, as actions speak louder than words.

Encourage Mindful Usage

Teach teens to use technology mindfully. They should pay attention to the time spent on different activities and how those activities make them feel. Just as a balanced food diet is about conscious choices, a digital diet seeks equilibrium.

Promote Offline Activities

Advocate for a balance between screen time and offline activities like physical exercise, reading, hobbies, or time spent in nature. It's akin to enriching a diet with a variety of nutrients.

Use Parental Control Tools

Consider parental control tools to monitor and limit screen time. These tools should be a last resort, used with your teen's knowledge and consent. The aim is to guide, not police, their digital interactions.

Managing screen time isn't about demonizing technology but helping teenagers use it to enhance their lives. The goal is for them to navigate this world with confidence and ease, reaping the benefits while mitigating the risks.

Balancing Offline and Online Lives

It's easy for teens to get swept up in the digital current: scrolling through social media, binge-watching videos, gaming, or staying constantly connected through messaging apps. But while technology is an unavoidable part of their lives, it's important to remind them (and ourselves) that life doesn't only happen on a screen.

This balance is crucial. While the digital world offers connection, entertainment, and even learning, it's just one part of the whole. The offline world, such as cooking a new recipe, painting just for fun, journaling, playing an instrument, brings depth. These moments foster confidence, self-expression, and the kind of joy that doesn't depend on likes or shares.

Even quiet, seemingly unproductive things like daydreaming, kicking a ball around, or lying in the grass watching clouds have their place. They give teens the mental space they don't always realize they need. In a world that's always on, the value of slowing down can't be overstated.

Implementing a Digital Detox: Practical Approaches

Helping your teenager take a break from screens doesn't have to feel like starting a war. With the right approach, it can be a gentle shift toward healthier habits.

Here are some practical tips to support a more balanced relationship with technology:

Schedule Tech-Free Time

Designate specific periods each week as tech-free, for example, during meals, an hour before bedtime, or an unplugged day over the weekend.

Encourage Engaging Offline Pursuits

Inspire your teenager to take part in offline activities they enjoy, such as arts and crafts, sports, music, or cooking. Assist them in discovering activities that bring both joy and fulfillment.

Set a Positive Example

Demonstrate positive digital usage habits. Let your teenager observe you reading a book, gardening, or pursuing a hobby, to set a solid example of the value and enjoyment of offline activities.

Establish a Tech-Free Zone

Create designated tech-free zones in your home, be it the dining table, the living room, or a cozy reading nook.

As your teen works on striking this balance, they'll gradually learn that life isn't about the number of likes on a post or the high score in a video game. It's about the simple joys and life, in all its beauty, should be experienced both online and offline.

EFFECTIVE COMMUNICATION WITH YOUR TEEN

An Art Worth Mastering

"There's one thing you can start doing right now that will change how you communicate with any young human: Remember what it's like to be one."

— Justin Young

There's one incredibly simple yet powerful switch you can flip, and it has the potential to completely transform the way you connect with the younger generation. This is all about taking a stroll down memory lane, back to the days when you were experiencing the twists and turns of adolescence. Yes, this is the secret sauce—rekindling that empathy by tapping into your own past.

I mean, let's be real. Remembering what it's like to be a young human isn't just a trip down nostalgia lane; it's a game-changer in how you communicate and relate to your teen. That's what Justin Young captures so perfectly in the quote above. When we take the time to reflect on our own teenage years, we don't just become better listeners—we become more understanding, more patient, and more present. We remember what it felt like not to be understood, and from there, real communication begins.

We all know that talking to teenagers isn't always straightforward. They might not say much, or say it in a way that sounds like they don't care. But behind the sighs, the sarcasm, and the silences, there's a whole emotional world. Understanding this world takes intention and effort.

In this chapter, we'll explore what it really means to communicate with your teen, not from a place of control, but from a place of connection. We'll dive into tools that help open the door: active listening, creating safe spaces for conversation, and knowing when to talk and when to hold space.

And as you read through this chapter, remember that communicating with your teen isn't about getting every word right. It's about showing up with warmth, respect, and a willingness to see the world through their eyes, even just a little.

Listening versus Hearing

Let's talk about something pretty powerful—the art of *really* listening. Not just hearing the words, but actually tuning in and really understanding what's going on.

Picture this: your teen flops onto the couch after school, phone in hand. You ask how their day was, and all you get is a quick, "fine." Seems like a simple, surface-level exchange, right? But if you pay attention, there's a whole silent conversation happening. The slouch, the quiet tone, no eye contact, those are the subtle signals giving you a glimpse into what they're actually feeling. Maybe they bombed a test, had a fight with a friend, or are just buried in school stress. It's like they're speaking in a quiet emotional code, and if you're really listening, you'll catch it.

Now, when they *do* start talking, maybe about why they skipped out on chores or came home late, try this small but powerful move: reflect their words back to them in your own way. If they say, "I couldn't do the dishes, I had to study for a test," you might respond, "Okay, so studying took priority and the dishes didn't get done."

Why does this help? It shows them you're not just half-listening, you're genuinely trying to understand. It also gives them a chance to clarify if you misunderstood something. It's like asking them indirectly, "Is this what you meant?" It keeps the conversation open and clear.

And here's another thing—avoid interrupting. Even if you want to jump in with advice or your own take, hold off and let them finish. That small act of patience shows respect, and it makes them far more likely to keep sharing.

In a world full of noise and distractions, real listening can feel like a lost art. But especially with teens, it's a skill that makes a difference, switching scattered exchanges to real conversations. You'll build trust, strengthen your connection, and create a space where they feel heard and safe.

Navigating Teenage Time Bombs

Identifying Triggers

Picture this: it's a calm afternoon, and you casually ask your teen to help out with a few chores. Suddenly, there's an explosion: raised voices, eye rolls, maybe even a door slam. This is the unpredictable world of teenage meltdowns: what we might call "teenage time bombs." And like with any ticking device, the key to avoiding detonation is knowing what sets it off.

These emotional flare-ups don't happen randomly. They're often sparked by very specific triggers: academic stress, social pressures, or even things that seem small to us, like a delayed Wi-Fi connection or an offhand comment about their laundry. It's important to remember that what feels minor to you might feel huge to them. Their world is intense, and their emotional landscape is still under construction.

Start by paying close attention to patterns. Does tension rise around exam time? After hanging out with certain friends? When they haven't had enough sleep? These patterns can reveal the stress points that make your teen more vulnerable to emotional outbursts.

Understanding these triggers doesn't mean we can prevent every blow-up, but it does give us a powerful tool—empathy. When we know what's underneath the surface, we're better prepared to respond with calm and compassion instead of frustration.

Now, let's break down some of the most common triggers and how to navigate them:

- **Academic Stress**

We had covered this in detail earlier, but it's worth mentioning as a possible trigger. Exam season, with its looming deadlines and mounting pressure, is a major trigger for many teens. The fear of failure and the intense expectations—whether from themselves, school, or home—can feel overwhelming. When the stakes feel high, even a small academic hiccup can spark a big emotional reaction.

- **Social Dynamics**

Friendships during adolescence can be a minefield. A comment taken the wrong way, feeling excluded, peer pressure, or drama within a friend group can create a swirl of emotions. Since social belonging is so important at this stage, anything that threatens that sense of connection can easily become a trigger.

- **Emotional Exhaustion**

Teenagers often juggle more than we realize—school, friendships, home responsibilities, identity struggles, and sometimes even part-time jobs or family issues. Over time, this can lead to emotional burnout. Without enough downtime or emotional space to process everything, even a small frustration can push them over the edge.

As parents or educators, recognizing patterns—like tension around certain subjects, shifts in behavior before exams, or signs of sleep deprivation—can help us step in with support before things escalate.

Encouraging breaks, offering a calm listening ear, and helping create a balanced routine can go a long way.

Calm and Composed Responses

When faced with these emotional explosions, resist the urge to match anger with anger. Fire fuels fire, escalating the conflict. Instead, respond with calmness and composure. Maintain a serene demeanor, not to suppress your emotions, but to manage them effectively. This creates a safe space where your teen feels heard, not attacked. Take a deep breath, keep your voice steady, and address the behavior without criticism.

Let's say you're a teacher, and during a class discussion, a student named Becky unexpectedly expresses frustration about the difficulty of the topic, resulting in a heated outburst. In this situation, the initial reaction might be to meet Becky's frustration with your frustration, creating a potentially volatile atmosphere in the classroom. However, applying the principle of calm and composed responses can significantly alter the dynamics:

Recognizing the Trigger

First, acknowledge that the challenging topic triggered Becky emotional response. It could be academic stress or a struggle to comprehend the material.

Calm and Composed Reaction

Instead of reacting with frustration or irritation, respond with calmness and composure. Keep your voice steady, take a moment to collect your thoughts, and then address Becky's concerns.

Empathetic Listening

Create a safe space by actively listening to Becky's frustrations. This doesn't mean agreeing with everything she says, but rather demonstrating that her feelings are acknowledged and respected.

Problem-Solving Approach

Whenever emotions run high, try to gently guide the moment toward problem-solving. Talk through the situation together and explore possible ways to handle it. Offer your support without judgment. Responding with calm and steadiness doesn't mean brushing feelings aside—it means helping your teen manage them in a healthier way.

This kind of response creates a safe, supportive environment where they feel heard and understood. It also models emotional regulation in action, showing them how to face challenges constructively rather than reactively.

Let's continue with our earlier example involving Becky. After she reacts with frustration during a challenging lesson, and you've responded with calm and empathy, the next step is to guide the moment toward a solution together.

Here's how that can look in practice:

Acknowledging Emotions

Begin by validating what Becky is feeling. This doesn't mean agreeing with everything she says—it just means showing her that her emotions are understood. You might say, "I can see this topic is really frustrating right now. It's okay to feel overwhelmed—these moments happen to all of us."

This kind of acknowledgment helps her feel seen rather than shut down.

Transition to Problem-Solving

Once her emotions have been acknowledged, gently pivot the conversation. A calm, open-ended question can do wonders: *"Do you want to talk about which part is feeling the hardest right now?"* or *"What do you think would make this feel more manageable?"* This shifts the focus from what went wrong to what can be done next.

Offering Strategies

Collaboratively explore possible ways forward. You might suggest:

- Breaking the task into smaller, more doable steps
- Revisiting earlier material she felt confident with
- Using visual aids, summaries, or examples that match her learning style

By brainstorming together, you're showing her how to move from stuck to supported without judgment.

Extra Help

Offer additional support if she needs more time or space to work through the material. You could say:

"If it would help, we can go over this one-on-one later, or I can give you some extra examples to try at your own pace."

This makes it clear that support is available without pressure.

Encourage Self-Advocacy

Remind her that asking for help is a strength, not a weakness. Try something like:

"If this happens again, don't be afraid to speak up—I'd rather we work through it together than let it build up."

You're reinforcing that her voice matters and that she has agency in the learning process.

Express Support

Close the conversation with a note of encouragement. Let her know you're on her side.

"You're not alone in this—I'm here to help you figure it out, and I believe you can."

Even a small, genuine comment like that can build a sense of safety and confidence.

This way, you're not just managing the moment; you're modeling emotional intelligence and resilience in real time. It's this kind of support that teaches them how to face challenges without fear and ask for help without shame.

Post-Conflict Resolution Follow-Ups

The resolution of a conflict isn't the end; what comes next matters just as much. Following up after the moment has passed gives teens a chance to reflect, process, and feel truly heard. Think of it as a quiet debrief after a storm: a time to check in, make sense of what happened, and consider what could be done differently next time.

Take Becky, for instance. After her emotional outburst and your calm, problem-solving conversation, things may have settled down. But don't let it end there. Maybe the next day, during a neutral moment, between classes, during lunch, or even just while walking out together, you gently check in:

Acknowledging the Resolution

Start by recognizing the effort she put into moving forward.

"Hey, I really appreciated how open you were yesterday. That took a lot of maturity."

This shows you noticed her growth, not just the disruption.

Transitioning to a Follow-Up Conversation

Keep the tone light and natural. No pressure, just curiosity and care.

"How did you feel about how we handled things yesterday? Did you find it helpful?"

Here, you're inviting her to reflect, not revisit the conflict.

Reflecting on the Experience

Ask open-ended questions that let her lead the reflection.

"Is there anything you'd do differently next time? Anything I could do differently?"

You're showing her that conflict resolution is a shared process, not a top-down directive.

Planning for Next Time

Discussing adjustments helps her feel more in control of future situations.

"If something like that comes up again, what would help you stay grounded?"

Maybe it's a signal word, a short break, or just knowing she won't be judged for having a tough moment.

Validating Her Feelings

Above all, remind her that her emotions are valid, even if the way they come out sometimes needs work.

"It's okay to have big feelings. What matters is how we move through them—and I'm here for that."

Turning Conflict into Growth

Let her know that these kinds of check-ins aren't about revisiting drama; they're about learning together. When teens know that their emotional moments won't be held against them, they start to feel safer and more open in the future.

Note that Becky's example can also be applied to parent-child relationships, not just teacher-student ones.

The Empathy Bridge

One of the most powerful ways to connect with your teen, especially during emotionally charged moments, is through empathy. When your teen is hurting, frustrated, or overwhelmed, they're not necessarily looking for solutions. What they often crave most is simple human understanding. They want to know they're not alone in what they're feeling. This is where building an "empathy bridge" comes in—small, intentional moments where you meet them emotionally, right where they are.

Let's see how you can do this in everyday moments:

Validating Feelings

Let's say your teen approaches you, upset that they didn't make the school basketball team. The natural instinct might be to comfort them with a hopeful, "You'll get it next year," or offer advice on what to improve. But what they often need first isn't reassurance—it's validation. A simple acknowledgment like, *"That must feel really disappointing. I can see how much this meant to you,"* goes a long way.

Validation says, *"I hear you. I see you. Your feelings are real, and they matter."* It's not about agreeing with everything they say or do; it's about honoring their emotional experience. Even if you can't fix the situation, showing that you understand how they feel builds trust and makes them more likely to open up again next time.

Sharing Personal Experiences

Another way to strengthen that bridge of empathy is by gently sharing your own experiences. When appropriate, opening up about times when you've felt let down or faced rejection helps normalize their emotions. Maybe you can recall a moment when you didn't get a job you really wanted, or when a big plan fell through.

Say something like, *"I remember being so crushed when I didn't get into the college I was hoping for. I know it's not the same, but I get what that kind of disappointment feels like."*

The point isn't to shift the focus to yourself, but to show them that you've been there, too.

Empathetic Responses

When your teen shares something difficult, resist the urge to jump into problem-solving mode. Instead, pause and reflect their feelings back with empathy. If they're upset about a fight with a friend, try: *"That sounds really painful. I can imagine you're feeling hurt and confused."*

Empathy says, *"I may not have all the answers, but I'm here with you."* It's about being emotionally present, not necessarily to fix, but to feel with them. These responses create a safe space where your teen knows they won't be dismissed, lectured, or rushed through their feelings.

You don't need dramatic speeches or the "right" words to build an empathy bridge. It's the small, consistent moments that add up. Each time you respond with presence and compassion, you lay down another brick. Over time, that bridge becomes strong enough to carry your connection through even the most turbulent teenage years.

DISCIPLINE AND BOUNDARIES

Guiding Your Teen With Empathy and **Consistency**

"Our boundaries define our personal space — and we need to be sovereign there in order to be able to step into our full power and potential."
~Jessica Moore

Jessica Moore's words beautifully capture what lies at the heart of healthy discipline and boundaries during the teen years. At its core, this is about more than just rules; it's about helping our teenagers feel safe enough to grow and strong enough to thrive.

Boundaries, when set with care and clarity, create a framework of trust and respect. They help define personal space, not to restrict or control, but to give room for autonomy and healthy development. For teenagers, whose brains are still learning how to self-regulate and make decisions, clear and respectful boundaries are the scaffolding for independence. They give teens something steady to push against as they figure out who they are.

That's where empathy comes in. It's not just about laying down rules—it's about listening to your teen's perspective and honoring their emotional world while still maintaining your role as a guide. Empathy doesn't mean letting go of structure; it means enforcing it in a way that respects the teenager's voice and humanity. It's saying, *"I hear you, and I understand, but here's why this boundary matters."*

Just as important as empathy is consistency. Boundaries that change from day to day or are enforced only when we're tired or angry send mixed messages. Teens need to know what to expect. When limits are predictable and fair, it creates stability, and from that, a sense of security. Even when they push back (and they will), consistency reassures them that the world around them isn't shifting beneath their feet.

In this chapter, we'll see how to guide teens with a combination of empathy and firmness. We'll look at how setting boundaries can actually strengthen your connection rather than weaken it and how consistent, respectful discipline builds the inner scaffolding your teen needs to step confidently into their power and potential.

Setting Boundaries and Building Consistency for Growth

Clear Expectations

Provide specific, detailed guidelines for tasks like chores, homework, curfew, and screen time.

Instead of vague instructions, offer clear and detailed expectations. For example, "Wash the dishes every evening after dinner and take out the trash every Tuesday and Friday morning."

Involvement and Collaboration

Involve your teenager in the process of setting expectations.

Encourage a conversation about what's reasonable, negotiable, and non-negotiable. This collaborative approach fosters a sense of value and increases their willingness to adhere to the rules.

Consistency as the Backbone

Now, let's talk about the backbone of it all – consistency. Without it, your efforts will be futile. Make sure to enforce rules consistently to avoid confusion or rule-bending. For instance, if washing dishes is a daily routine, stick to it consistently, not just when it's convenient.

Address Rule Violations Promptly

Promptly address any rule violations, irrespective of external factors.

Consistent enforcement sends a strong message about the importance of rules and the need for respect.

Regular Revisions

As your teenager matures, regularly revise and update boundaries.

Adjust rules to reflect your teen's growing maturity and expanding responsibilities. This ongoing process respects their evolving individuality and maintains a harmonious living environment.

This isn't about letting go of all the rules; it's about adjusting to make sure the rules still apply.

Deliberate and Thoughtful Construction

Each boundary is a deliberate and thoughtful construction.

It lays the foundation for a healthy parent-teenager relationship by shaping their understanding of respect, responsibility, and the value of clear guidelines.

Overall, setting boundaries isn't about power plays or strict rules; it's about building a clear, consistent, and adaptable framework to guide your teenager's behavior.

Navigating the Discipline Dilemma

When parenting teenagers, the age-old adage "Spare the rod, spoil the child" may not hold water. Dealing with teenage misbehavior requires a nuanced and empathetic approach — a shift from punishment to consequences.

Natural Consequences

- Scenario: Your teenager consistently forgets to set their alarm, leading to waking up late and missing the bus. Instead of a reprimand, consider letting natural consequences unfold. They miss the bus; they must figure out alternative travel, facing any repercussions from the school administration.

- Essence: Natural consequences provide learning opportunities, allowing teenagers to understand that their choices have consequences.

Logical Consequences

- Scenario: Your teenager borrows your car without asking and gets a speeding ticket. Instead of solely relying on natural consequences, implement logical consequences. For instance, temporarily restrict their driving privileges or have them pay the ticket from their savings.

- Essence: Logical consequences are directly linked to misbehavior, but implemented by you — they are respectful, relevant, and realistic.

Avoiding Punitive Measures

In the heat of the moment, punitive measures like grounding or taking away privileges may be tempting.

- Concern: Punitive measures can breed resentment, damage your relationship, and fail to teach your teen about responsibility and decision-making.
- Alternative: Instead of punishing, focus on teaching. Use misbehavior as a teaching moment, guiding your teen towards better choices.

The Power of Choice

By allowing natural and logical consequences to unfold, you empower your teen to make choices and be accountable for them.

- Message: "I trust you to make decisions and handle the consequences." This fosters responsibility, boosts self-esteem, and enhances decision-making skills.
- Role: Your role is not to control but to guide, support, and allow freedom for learning from choices.

Discipline as a Learning Journey

Navigating teen discipline can be simple.

- Approach: Focus on natural and logical consequences, avoid punitive measures, and foster choice and accountability.
- Outcome: Transform discipline complications into a learning journey that shapes behavior and strengthens your relationship with your teen.

Navigating Defiance

When it comes to parenting teens, few things can feel more frustrating—or more personal—than dealing with defiance. It's one of those challenges that can catch you off guard, even when you think you're prepared. It's like caring for a wilting plant: the leaves droop, the color fades, and nothing seems to help. But the real fix doesn't lie in trimming the edges; it lies in getting to the roots.

Understanding the Root Cause

Defiance in teens is rarely just about the surface behavior. Sometimes, it's a cry for independence. Other times, it's about pushing boundaries, expressing bottled-up frustration, or trying to feel heard. And quite often, as we saw earlier, there's something else simmering beneath: school stress, social drama, or a growing sense of feeling misunderstood or overwhelmed.

When we take the time to look past the behavior and ask what's driving it, we can stop reacting and start responding with intention.

Responding Without Escalating

Defiance can easily turn into a tug-of-war—one where both sides dig in, and no one really wins. When your teen pushes, your first instinct might be to push back. But what if you didn't? What if, instead of grabbing the rope tighter, you simply let go?

Staying calm in those heated moments isn't easy, but it's powerful. It shows your teen that you're not there to battle them—you're there to understand. Taking a deep breath, speaking gently, and focusing on the behavior (not their character) can shift the entire energy of the conversation.

Using "I" statements can also go a long way. Rather than saying, *"You're being rude,"* try something like, *"I feel dismissed when my requests are ignored."* This small shift takes the sting out of confrontation and opens the door to actual connection. It invites your teen into the conversation instead of pushing them further away.

When to Seek Professional Help

There are times when love, patience, and calm communication still don't seem to be enough—and that's okay.

Just like you'd call in a gardener if your entire garden was struggling, it's completely valid to seek help if your teen's behavior seems overwhelming or persistent. If defiance is showing up alongside aggression, risky behavior, or signs of depression or self-harm, it's time to consider involving a professional.

Therapists and counselors can offer a neutral, supportive space for your teen to unpack what they're going through. More importantly, they can equip both you and your teen with tools to navigate tough moments in healthier, more constructive ways.

As a parent or caregiver, it's important to note that reaching out for help isn't a sign of failure—it's an act of strength. It means you're doing everything in your power to support your teen, even if it means letting someone else take the reins.

Opportunities for Growth and Connection

While defiance can feel like a brick wall, it can also be a doorway to deepen your connection. These challenges, hard as they may be, offer us the chance to show up for our teens—not with lectures or ultimatums, but with steadiness, empathy, and presence. They are opportunities for you to reinforce your love, model emotional regulation, and remind your teen that they're not alone, even when things feel tense or messy.

Next, we'll shift our focus to another key part of their world—academics. We've touched on this a bit in previous chapters as a stressor. However, here we will explore how the teenage brain processes learning, what fuels or hinders motivation, and how we can support their academic journey in a way that feels grounded, healthy, and empowering.

THE LEARNING SCOPE

Helping Your Teen Towards Academic Success

"Only those who dare to fail greatly can ever achieve greatly."
– Robert F. Kennedy

As a parent helping your teen navigate the ups and downs of academic life, these words from Robert F. Kennedy hold powerful truth. They are a reminder we all need sometimes, especially when we're watching our teens wrestle with pressure, setbacks, and the constant demand to succeed.

The path to academic success can be messy. It includes late nights, missed marks, second tries, and unexpected detours. And that's okay. In fact, it's more than okay; it's essential. The ability to take risks, to try and fail and try again, is what builds not just knowledge, but confidence, resilience, and grit. Your teen may stumble, yes—but those stumbles often become the very ground they'll rise from.

One of the most meaningful gifts you can give your teenager is permission to fail. Not the kind of failure that comes from carelessness; but the kind that comes from pushing their boundaries, challenging themselves, and daring to try something new. Whether it's taking on a difficult subject, experimenting with a different study method, or simply asking for help when they're stuck, these moments are where real growth happens.

Reframing failure as part of the learning process—not as something to fear, but something to learn from— is key. It allows your teen to see challenges not as dead ends but as stepping stones. It also signals to them that success isn't just about grades; it's about perseverance, curiosity, and learning.

This chapter dives into just that: how to support your teen through the academic journey with encouragement, strategy, and heart. We'll look at how motivation works, what drives learning, and how you can help them stay focused and resilient, even when things get hard.

And let's be real, motivation isn't always easy to come by, even for adults. That's why understanding what fuels your teen matters. One big driver? Intrinsic motivation. This is that inner spark that lights up when they're doing something because they genuinely enjoy it or find meaning in it. For them, it might be the thrill of solving a tough math problem, the satisfaction of finishing a great book, or that feeling of pride when they finally understand a tricky science concept.

These are the moments we want to nurture—not through pressure, but through support and encouragement.

How Can Parents Help?

Well, let me share with you some tips below:

- **Be a Learning Ally**

Act as a learning ally for your teenager. Show interest in what they're studying, ask about their projects, and be there to answer questions or help when they're stuck. When they see that you're genuinely interested, it can boost their motivation.

- **Create a Study Routine**

Help your teenager establish a study routine. Consistency is key. Having a set time and place for studying can make it a habit, and habits are easier to stick with. Make sure they have a quiet and comfortable space to focus.

- **Explore Different Learning Styles**

People learn in different ways. Some are visual learners, some prefer reading, and others learn by doing. Figure out your teen's learning style and encourage them to use techniques that suit them best. This could include visual aids, flashcards, or hands-on activities.

- **Encourage Breaks and Self-Care**

Studying for long hours without breaks can lead to burnout. Encourage your teenager to take short breaks, stretch, or do something enjoyable between study sessions. Taking care of their well-being is crucial for long-term success.

- **Connect Learning to Real Life**

Help your teen see the real-world applications of what they're learning. Whether it's math, science, or literature, show them how these subjects relate to everyday life. Understanding the practical aspects can make studying more meaningful and interesting.

- **Offer Choices and Autonomy**

Allow your teenager to have a say in their learning. Offer them choices when possible, like letting them pick a topic for a project or decide how to approach a particular assignment. Autonomy can increase their sense of responsibility and motivation.

- **Seek External Support**

If your teenager is struggling with a particular subject, consider seeking external support. This could be a tutor, a study group, or online resources. Sometimes, a different perspective or additional help can make a significant difference.

- **Set a Positive Example**

Children often learn by example. If they see you valuing learning, setting goals, and celebrating your achievements, it sets a positive tone. Share your own experiences of overcoming challenges and emphasize the importance of continuous learning.

Remember, the key is to create a supportive and engaging environment where learning is seen as a positive and rewarding experience. By incorporating these additional points, you're setting the stage for your teenager's academic success and fostering a lifelong love of learning.

Smart Work Over Hard Work

Not all effort is created equal, and when it comes to schoolwork, the secret isn't always working harder, but working smarter. Many teens believe that long hours spent bent over a book equals success, but what really matters is *how* they study. This is where you, as a parent, can make a meaningful difference.

Helping your teen develop effective study habits doesn't mean micromanaging their homework. It means guiding them toward techniques that not only make learning more manageable but also more enjoyable.

For instance:

Effective Note-Taking

Taking notes isn't just about copying everything the teacher says. It's about picking out the most important ideas and capturing them in a way that actually makes sense to the learner. Encourage your teen to experiment with different note-taking methods, whether it's outlining ideas in a sequence, using the Cornell Method (dividing the page into keywords, notes, and a summary), or drawing out mind maps.

The goal is for their notes to reflect how *they* understand the topic, not just how it was presented. Support them by asking questions like, *"Which method helps you remember better?"* or *"Want to show me how you organized that tricky topic?"* Even this simple interest from you reinforces the value of finding a system that works.

Remind them, too, that notes aren't just for storing information—they're tools for making connections. Encourage them to highlight, doodle, rephrase ideas in their own words—anything that brings the material to life. Their notebook doesn't need to be perfect—it needs to make sense to *them*.

Active Recall

Passive review—just re-reading notes—only goes so far. Active recall, on the other hand, is a game-changer. It's like watching a mystery movie and trying to remember the clues without rewinding. It requires the brain to work a little harder, and that's exactly what helps the learning stick.

Encourage your teen to quiz themselves, summarize what they've just learned out loud, or even explain it to you as if they were teaching a class. (Bonus: this can be a fun way to connect, too.) Flashcards are a great tool here, as is turning headings in their notes into questions.

Spaced Repetition

You know how watering a plant once a month won't keep it alive, but a little bit every few days does the trick? The same goes for studying. Spaced repetition is the habit of reviewing material over increasing intervals, rather than cramming it all in the night before a test.

Help your teen build this rhythm by checking in after they've learned something new. Maybe say, *"Hey, want to do a quick review of what you covered yesterday?"* Then revisit it again a few days later. There are even apps that can help space out review sessions based on how well your teen remembers each item.

By revisiting content over time, their brain has a better chance of turning short-term knowledge into long-term understanding.

Time Management

One of the biggest hurdles teens face isn't always the material itself; it's knowing how to manage their time. You can help by guiding them to break their work into smaller, doable chunks. Sit down together and create a flexible schedule that makes space for each subject, built around realistic goals and built-in breaks.

Techniques like the Pomodoro Method—25 minutes of focused work followed by a 5-minute break—can make studying feel less overwhelming. And remember, time off *is* part of smart work. Encourage them to step away from the screen, take a walk, stretch, or grab a snack.

Rather than enforcing a strict timetable, help them build a relationship with time that feels empowering instead of draining.

The Failure Fallacy

Growth Mindset

We often think of failure as the opposite of success, but in reality, it's one of the most powerful tools for learning. Helping your teen embrace a *growth mindset* means encouraging them to see intelligence and ability not as fixed traits, but as things they can develop with effort, time, and persistence.

A growth mindset invites your teen to look at challenges and setbacks as stepping stones, not signs that they're "not good enough," but proof that they're learning and growing. Instead of saying, "I failed the test," they can begin to say, "I didn't do well this time, but I'll learn from it and do better next time." It's a subtle shift, but one that can completely change how they view themselves and their potential.

Seeing Mistakes as Opportunities

When your teen stumbles during a class presentation or struggles with a tough subject, their first instinct might be frustration or self-doubt. This is where you can gently step in and help reframe the moment. Mistakes aren't proof of failure—they're part of the process.

You might say something like, *"Okay, that didn't go the way you hoped—but what do you think you could try differently next time?"* Over time, they'll learn that one misstep doesn't define them. It's just feedback for their next step.

Constructive Feedback

Feedback is powerful—but how it's delivered makes all the difference. Try to focus less on the outcome ("You got an A!") and more on the process that got them there. Say things like, "You put in consistent study time and stayed focused—that really paid off."

When they're struggling, offer feedback that's specific and supportive rather than vague or critical. Instead of "You need to do better," try, "I noticed you got stuck on the last few questions—let's figure out where it got confusing and work through it together."

This kind of feedback shows them that learning is a process, and improvement is always possible.

Building Resilience

Sometimes, things don't go as planned—and that's okay. What matters most is how your teen bounces back. Resilience is what helps them push through frustration, setbacks, or even failure, and keep moving forward.

Help them develop resilience by normalizing struggle. Remind them it's okay to feel disappointed—but it's also okay to start again. Teach simple tools like taking a break, deep breathing, or walking away for a moment and coming back with fresh eyes (review our section on resilience for more tips on how to do this). Encourage them to ask for help—from teachers, peers, or even you—when they're stuck.

Remember that when you support your teen in developing a growth mindset, you're not just helping them succeed in school. You're helping them build the emotional and mental tools they'll need for life.

THE INVISIBLE BATTLES OF ADOLESCENCE

Body Image, Peer Pressure, and Impulsivity

"To lose confidence in one's body is to lose confidence in oneself."

~Simone de Beauvoir.

During the teenage years, when so much of a young person's identity is still taking shape, this quote really hits hard. Adolescence is a time of massive physical, emotional, and social shifts. As teens become more aware of how they look and how they're perceived, their relationship with their body can start to define how they feel about themselves as a whole.

Body image can become a quiet battlefield. Teens are constantly bombarded with messages, online, at school, and even from friends, about what's considered "good enough." And when those standards feel out of reach, it's not just about appearances anymore. Their confidence, sense of identity, and self-worth can take a hit too.

Then there's peer pressure. It's not always loud or evident; it can be subtle, like the pressure to dress a certain way, follow certain trends, or keep up with filtered versions of reality they see on social media. The desire to fit in during this time is so strong, and for some teens, this desire can override their better judgment or push them into decisions that don't align with who they truly are.

Now, when you add impulsivity to the mix, it's easy to see how quickly things can snowball. One impulsive choice, made in the heat of wanting to be accepted or seen, can lead to unhealthy habits like crash dieting, excessive exercising, or even riskier behaviors.

But teens don't have to fight these battles alone. As parents, caregivers, and educators, we can be their safe harbor; the place where they learn to see their body with kindness, where their worth isn't tied to how they look, and where fitting in doesn't mean losing themselves. We can start by having real conversations about body image and self-acceptance. We can help them question unrealistic standards and tune into what makes them unique.

The goal isn't to shield them from the world—they'll face pressures, no doubt—but to equip them with the tools and self-awareness to move through it without losing their grounding. Helping them build a positive, respectful relationship with their body doesn't just boost confidence—it lays the groundwork for a strong, steady sense of self that can weather the ups and downs of adolescence and beyond.

Let's see how to do this in this chapter:

Navigating the Teen Body Image Maze–For Parents

We know that being a teenager is like being in a funhouse mirror maze – nothing looks quite right, everything feels exaggerated, and it's easy to get disoriented. On top of juggling school, friendships, and growing responsibilities, your teen is also trying to figure out how they feel about their body—and that's no small feat in a world constantly telling them how they *should* look.

As a parent, it can be hard to know how to help. But here's the good news: you don't need to have all the answers. You just need a few solid tools and the willingness to stay in the conversation. Think of this as a heart-to-heart over coffee (or tea), where we unpack three powerful ways to support your teen through the body image maze: media literacy, positive self-talk, and the impact of representation and role models.

Media Literacy

Social media is like a non-stop slideshow of seemingly perfect bodies, flawless faces, and jet-setting lifestyles. But here's the deal: those images are often as real as unicorns. Media literacy is like putting on reality-check glasses; it helps your teen see behind the polished façade.

What can you do?

Teach your teen to question what they see on social media. Explain how photo editing apps create fantasy, and how advertising preys on insecurities to sell products. Make them media-savvy so they can look at these images with a critical eye. This empowers them to appreciate diversity, knowing that worth isn't determined by appearance.

Positive Self-Talk

What your teen says to themselves matters a lot. This internal dialogue is called self-talk, and it's a powerful tool in building a positive body image.

What can you do?

Encourage positive self-talk. Help your teen recognize and replace negative thoughts with affirmations that focus on strengths, abilities, and character rather than just appearance. Remind them that everyone is unique, with qualities that go beyond physical looks. This builds a foundation for self-acceptance and self-love.

Role Models and Representation

Positive role models are those who reflect diverse, realistic, and unaltered bodies and appearances. These role models, both in real life and the media, provide a counter-narrative to the narrow beauty standards bombarding your teen.

What can you do?

Encourage your teen to find role models who celebrate body positivity, diversity, and self-acceptance. It could be athletes emphasizing strength and health over appearance, celebrities speaking out against body shaming, or influencers sharing unedited photos. These role models show that beauty isn't confined to a particular size or shape, and looks don't determine success.

Navigating the Peer Pressure Puzzle- For Parents

In this part of our book, we'll tackle the social maze of peer pressure. Teenagers face a horde of influences, and it's essential to equip them with the right tools to navigate these challenging waters.

Assertiveness Skills

Assertiveness helps your teen stand up for themselves while respecting others. This skill involves expressing feelings, opinions, and needs confidently. It's like giving your teen a sturdy boat to navigate through the waves of peer pressure.

What can you do?

Guide your teenager to communicate assertively. Practice scenarios together, like saying no to risky behaviors or standing up against bullying. Reinforce that it's absolutely okay to go against the crowd and express disagreement respectfully. Like any skill, assertiveness improves with practice.

Choosing Friends Wisely

Encourage your teen to be mindful of their friends—do these friends respect their values? Are they accepted for who they are? True friendships uplift; they don't bring anyone down.

What can you do?

Ask reflective questions. Are their friends positively influencing them? Do these friendships contribute to their growth? Urge your teen to hold onto friendships that value authenticity and mutual growth. Remind them that friendships should never compromise their values or well-being.

Family Values and Personal Beliefs

Family values provide guidance in the vastness of adolescence. Engage in open discussions about your family values, such as honesty, respect, responsibility, and compassion. Explain why these values matter and how they can steer your teen's decisions.

What can you do?

Encourage your teen to reflect on their personal beliefs. What do they stand for? What principles guide their actions? This introspection strengthens their moral compass, helping them navigate peer pressure without losing sight of their values.

Guiding Teens Through Impulsivity

Now, let's talk about helping your teens hit the brakes on impulsivity and cruise through life with a bit more control and patience:

Delayed Gratification

Picture your teen scrolling through their favorite online store. They've just spotted a pair of sneakers they really want—but they've also been saving up for something bigger, like concert tickets or a new phone. Now they're stuck in that classic tug-of-war: do they hit "Buy Now" for that quick thrill, or keep saving for the thing they've been dreaming about?

Choosing the latter is where delayed gratification comes to life. It's not about denying pleasure altogether; it's about learning when to pause, weigh the options, and hold out for something more meaningful. And in today's world of instant everything, helping your teen build this skill is a powerful step toward long-term resilience and self-control.

What can you do?

Start simple. Engage your teen in activities that require waiting, like baking a cake. Waiting for it to bake and cool before diving in is a small lesson in patience. As they get better at waiting, introduce larger goals that demand more extended periods of self-control. This cultivates patience, stress management, and better decision-making.

Role-Playing Scenarios

Let's say your teen wants to attend a late-night party, and you're concerned about their safety. You can switch gears and role-play this scenario together. Take turns playing both sides.

This exercise helps your teen explore different ways to handle situations, express their thoughts and feelings, and understand your perspective.

Navigating the Dark Side of the Internet

The digital world is expansive, and as expected, not all online interactions are friendly. There's a shadowy side—an alleyway concealed where cyberbullying lurks. This form of bullying takes place behind screen names and profile pictures, making it challenging to detect.

Recognizing Signs of Cyberbullying

If your teenager appears distressed after using their devices, becomes secretive about online activities, or exhibits changes in behavior like withdrawing from friends and family, it might be a sign of cyberbullying. Other indicators include alterations in eating or sleeping patterns, declining grades, or sudden disinterest in school.

Impact on Mental Health

Cyberbullying triggers feelings of sadness, fear, and loneliness. It can lead to a struggle to focus, with hurtful comments or threatening messages lingering in their thoughts. The impact on mental health can be profound, potentially causing or exacerbating issues like anxiety, depression, and even suicidal thoughts.

In the next section, we will see the effects of adolescent pressures in action and how to go around them.

Case Studies and Solutions

Real-World Challenges

Cyberbullying

Consider Ben, a high school sophomore targeted by an anonymous online hate page. Recognizing the signs, Ben's parents took swift action, reporting the incident to the school and the social media platform. Professional counseling helped Ben navigate the emotional distress, emphasizing the importance of open communication, prompt action, and seeking professional help.

Academic Pressure

In Lisa's case, intense academic pressure led to panic attacks. Intervention from her parents and a school counselor provided stress management techniques, emphasizing the need for a balanced approach to academics, prioritizing learning over grades and well-being over achievements.

Substance Abuse

Andrew's early experimentation with drugs was met with calm but decisive intervention from his parents. They reached out for professional support and enrolled him in a peer support group.

His story highlights the importance of early intervention, professional help, and peer support in dealing with teenage substance abuse.

Mental Health Issues

On the other hand, Nina battled depression, concealed by typical teenage behavior. Recognizing the signs, Nina's family sought professional help. This emphasizes the importance of recognizing mental health issues, seeking professional help, and providing a supportive home environment.

As we move on to the next chapter, let's hold on to one thing: every challenge is a chance to connect with our teens, regardless of how "bad" the situation may seem.

EMBRACING UNIQUENESS

Navigating the Spectrum of Individual Differences in Adolescents

"Every one of us is different in some way, but for those of us who are more different, we have to put more effort into convincing the less different that we can do the same thing they can, just differently."
— Marlee Matlin

While everyone is different in their own way, those who stand out a little more, whether due to a disability, neurodivergence, cultural background, or any other reason, often carry the extra emotional labor of proving they belong. Not by changing who they are, but by showing that they too can thrive, just in their own way.

When it comes to teenagers, this truth takes on even more weight. Adolescence is a time of exploration, identity-shaping, and comparison. It's when many young people start to feel the pressure to fit into predefined boxes; boxes that may not have been made with them in mind. That's why creating a space where they feel accepted for who they *truly* are becomes not just helpful, but essential.

As parents, educators, and caregivers, part of our job is helping teens embrace their individuality, not as something to overcome, but as something to be proud of. It's about showing them that different doesn't mean less. That success doesn't have one look, one path, or one speed. And that their unique ways of thinking, learning, expressing, and being are not only valid, but valuable.

Fostering this kind of inclusive mindset starts with simple, consistent actions: listening without judgment, celebrating effort over comparison, and reminding teens that there are many ways to be smart, talented, kind, and capable. When we create a culture where differences are welcomed and respected, we offer our teenagers the freedom to grow into the fullest version of themselves without needing to shrink or stretch to meet someone else's expectations.

Let's see how:

Embracing Individuality

Here, we'll take a closer look at what it means to be "normal" (hint: it's not one-size-fits-all). Teenagers aren't meant to be carbon copies of each other — they're a mix of temperaments, talents, quirks, and questions, each one unfolding in their own time. Appreciating their differences is necessary if we want to truly connect with and support them. Each teen is a one-of-a-kind masterpiece, still in the making.

Personality Traits

Teenagers, like stars in a vast sky, shine with distinct personality traits. Some may lean towards introversion, finding solace in quiet introspection, while others radiate extroversion, thriving in the energy of social interactions. When it comes to education, organizational wizards coexist with spontaneous thinkers.

What can you do?

Appreciate these traits as windows into their world. By understanding their behavior, preferences, and interaction styles, we can guide them in a way that resonates with their unique personality.

Learning Styles

Just as we savor different tastes in music or food, teenagers have diverse learning styles. Visual learners absorb knowledge through images and diagrams, auditory learners thrive in discussions and lectures, while kinesthetic learners flourish through hands-on activities.

What can you do?

Recognize and embrace their learning style. Tailor teaching or parenting strategies to match their preferences, enriching their learning experience and enhancing understanding and retention of information.

Emotional Sensitivities

As we now understand, emotions in adolescence are unpredictable and diverse. Some teenagers experience emotions intensely, while others maintain a steady emotional landscape. Recognizing these emotional sensitivities allows us to understand their emotional climate and support them accordingly.

What can you do?

Acknowledge and validate their feelings. Understanding their emotional experiences enables us to provide the necessary support, manage emotional outbursts, and navigate conflicts with sensitivity.

Social Preferences

Teenagers, social explorers in their own right, showcase diverse social preferences. Some embrace large gatherings, while others seek comfort in intimate settings.

What can you do?

Consider social preferences as a roadmap to their social world. Respect their comfort zones, offer guidance in building positive social relationships, and provide support in overcoming social challenges. This knowledge unveils insights into their behavior, fostering a deeper connection.

Navigating Diverse Personality Types

When it comes to personalities, teenagers come with a rich category of traits. To guide them effectively, let's have a look at strategies tailored to different personality types:

Strategies for Introverted Teens

Introverted teenagers recharge through solitude, valuing depth in social interactions. Connect with introverted teens by respecting their need for personal space and quiet time. Avoid labeling them as shy, appreciate their reflective nature, and engage in meaningful one-on-one conversations. Also, support their deep interests, allowing their thoughts and ideas to speak volumes.

Strategies for Extroverted Teens

An extroverted teenager thrives in social circles, enjoying group activities and lively conversations. Embrace their social nature by providing opportunities for expression and engaging in stimulating discussions.

Encourage participation in group activities that align with their outgoing personality. While they seek external stimulation, help them find moments of quiet reflection, creating a balance between energetic social engagement and introspective solitude.

Strategies for Sensitive Teens

Sensitive teens are attuned to emotional nuances, empathetic, and deeply affected by others' feelings. Acknowledge their emotions without judgment, fostering a safe space for expression. Encourage creative outlets like art, music, or writing to channel their sensitivity positively. Make sure you recognize their strength in empathy and connection, so they are able to turn their emotional depth into a source of resilience and understanding.

Strategies for Assertive Teens

Assertive teens exude confidence, take initiative, and stand up for their beliefs. Respect their independence, supporting their self-expression and leadership qualities.

Where appropriate, provide constructive feedback and guide them in developing active listening skills and empathy. Take any chance you can get to channel their assertiveness positively, nurturing qualities that drive leadership, initiative, and positive change.

Case Study

Exploring the Impact of Individual Differences on Behavior

The Introverted Teen: Grace's Story

Grace is a 14-year-old introvert who cherishes alone time and thrives in one-on-one interactions. Grace's parents initially worried about her reserved nature, mistaking it for shyness or social anxiety.

Understanding the nuances of introversion, they came to appreciate Grace's deep reflective nature and her ability to connect on a profound level with a few close friends. Respecting her need for personal space, they supported her love for painting and reading, providing the joy and solitude she needed.

The Extroverted Teen: Liam's Journey

Liam, a 13-year-old extrovert, finds energy in social interactions and group activities. Initially, his parents found his constant need for social engagement exhausting. Recognizing this as part of his extroverted nature, they began to value his social skills and his knack for making friends easily.

Liam thrives when surrounded by people, and his parents support his extroverted tendencies by encouraging team sports and social events, providing the external stimulation he craves.

The Sensitive Teen: Maya's Emotional World

Maya, a 15-year-old with heightened emotional sensitivity, experiences emotions intensely. Her parents, initially overwhelmed by the depth of her reactions, learned to value her deep empathy and keen observance of others' feelings.

Recognizing Maya's rich inner life expressed through poetry, they supported her sensitivity by validating her emotions, creating a calm environment, and encouraging creative outlets for emotional expression.

The Assertive Teen: Ethan's Confidence Unleashed

Ethan, a 16-year-old assertive teenager, fearlessly expresses his thoughts and stands up for his beliefs. His parents initially found his assertiveness challenging, mistaking it for disobedience.

Understanding his assertive nature, they learned to appreciate his self-confidence and leadership qualities.

Ethan takes initiative in group projects and stands up against bullying. His parents support his assertiveness by fostering open communication, respecting his opinions, and guiding him to balance assertiveness with active listening and empathy.

These case studies highlight the diverse experiences of teenagers, emphasizing that understanding and supporting them require a personalized approach.

One of the most rewarding parts of parenting a teenager is watching them come into their own. Discovering their unique strengths is all about being keen enough to notice the little things that light them up.

The key is to tune into what draws them in. A teen who's always humming a tune or writing lyrics might be exploring a creative path in music. One who patiently helps their younger sibling with homework could be showing early signs of becoming a future teacher or mentor. Our job is to notice these sparks and gently fan them, without any pressure.

Of course, part of supporting growth also means acknowledging the areas where they struggle. This isn't about pointing out flaws; it's about recognizing where they might need a bit more guidance. Confidence doesn't grow from praise alone; it comes from trying, stumbling, and realizing you can get back up.

As we turn the page to the next chapter, we'll see how you can build a strong, trusting, and lasting connection with your teen.

11

BUILDING BRIDGES

Fostering a Meaningful Connection With Your Teen

"The way we talk to our children becomes their inner voice."

— Peggy O'Mara

There's something quietly powerful in the way we speak to our teenagers. Our tone, our choice of words, even the pauses between them, often shape how our teens talk to themselves. Peggy O'Mara's quote reminds us that what we say today remains in our children's hearts tomorrow.

Fostering a meaningful connection with your teen is essential. While teens may not always say it out loud, what they crave most is to feel understood, accepted, and deeply connected at home.

When that connection is strong, it becomes a grounding force. It helps your teen feel secure in who they are, believe in their worth, and bounce back from life's inevitable stumbles. And it doesn't take grand gestures. Often, it starts with small, everyday moments—listening without rushing, showing up without fixing, and choosing words that build up rather than break down.

In this chapter, we'll explore what it means to truly connect with your teenager. We'll look at how your daily interactions, no matter how brief, can become the foundation for trust, self-worth, and emotional resilience.

Nurturing Connection through the Power of Presence

Recall a moment when you engaged in a heartfelt conversation with a friend. Here, you weren't just hearing words but truly listening, understanding emotions, and connecting with experiences. This is the essence of active listening, a powerful tool in building a strong relationship with your teen.

Active Listening

Active listening involves

- Paying full attention: Set aside distractions, focus on what your teen is saying.
- Acknowledging feelings: Validate their experiences without judgment.
- Reflecting back: Confirm understanding, like saying, "So you're feeling overwhelmed with the project because you're not sure where to start."
- Asking open-ended questions: Encourage expression, like "How did that make you feel?" or "What do you think you could do in this situation?"

By practicing active listening, you communicate to your teen that their feelings matter, creating a safe space for open, honest communication, and building trust and respect.

Non-Judgmental Attitude

A non-judgmental attitude is an open door, inviting your teen to express themselves without fear of criticism. This involves:

- Respecting their feelings: Even if you don't fully understand or agree.

- Avoiding criticism: Instead of saying, "You're being dramatic," say, "I can see that this is really upsetting you."
- Accepting your teen: Respecting their individuality, interests, and unique perspective.

By adopting a non-judgmental attitude, you reinforce that your love and acceptance are unconditional, fostering a sense of security and belonging, and strengthening your connection.

Consistent Availability

Tips for consistent availability

- Make time for quality interactions: Share meals, hobbies, or casual chats.
- Emotional availability: Be ready to listen and provide comfort, especially during challenges.
- Express openness: Let your teen know they can talk to you about anything, anytime.

Consistent availability shows your teen that you're a reliable, trustworthy source of support. This fosters a sense of security, boosts confidence, and strengthens your bond, creating a foundation for a thriving parent-teen relationship.

Cultivating Connection in Everyday Moments with Quality Time

Shared Hobbies

Immerse yourself and your teen in a shared hobby – whether it's gardening, building model airplanes, or playing chess. Beyond the activity itself, these moments are about connection, understanding, and joy. Shared hobbies create a relaxed, pressure-free environment for interaction, allowing conversations to flow naturally. You get to see your teen in a different light, appreciate their skills and passions, and express your pride and admiration.

Regular Family Meals

Sharing a meal is a powerful tool for connection. It offers a consistent platform for communication, providing an opportunity to catch up on each other's days, discuss topics of interest, and share thoughts and feelings. So, gather your family around the dinner table, surrounded by the aroma of a home-cooked meal and the hum of conversation.

Weekend Outings

Consider weekend outings as adventures, an escape from usual routines. Whether it's a hike in the local park, a movie night, or a museum visit, these outings provide a change of scenery that can refresh and rejuvenate your relationship with your teen.

Parenting Styles

As we said, no two children are alike, and a one-size-fits-all parenting style doesn't apply. As parents, we must be flexible, adapting our approach to our teenager's unique needs, personality, and the situation. Let's explore three common parenting styles and their influence on our connection with teens.

Authoritative Style

Think of this as the "sweet spot" in parenting. Authoritative parents set clear expectations and boundaries, but they also listen. They encourage their teens to make choices and learn from them, within a safe structure.

It's not about micromanaging every decision but about being available with guidance, support, and firm-but-fair consequences when needed. Teens raised this way often feel respected, heard, and empowered, which can make all the difference during these emotionally complex years.

Permissive Style

It's natural to want to be close to your teen—to be someone they confide in, laugh with, and feel safe around. Permissive parents often lean into this role, offering warmth and openness, but sometimes at the cost of structure.

While it's beautiful to be a source of emotional safety, teens still need boundaries to feel secure. The key is balance: be a trusted friend *and* a steady guide. Show unconditional love, but don't shy away from saying no or stepping in when needed. Structure isn't the opposite of love—it's an expression of it.

Authoritarian Style

This style is more traditional: think clear rules, little negotiation, and a strong focus on discipline. While it might keep things orderly on the surface, it can sometimes create distance between you and your teen.

If you've leaned toward this approach, consider softening the edges. Invite your teen into conversations, ask for their input, and explain the "why" behind your expectations. Discipline doesn't have to mean control – it can be a way to teach, to guide, and to build mutual respect. Teens respond far better when they feel seen and included, not just directed.

Building and Sustaining Trust

Creating a strong foundation of trust with your teen doesn't happen overnight. It's something that builds slowly through your words, your actions, and how you show up when it matters.

Let's explore what it looks like to nurture this kind of trust in practical, heartfelt ways:

Honesty and Transparency

Being honest with your teen doesn't mean telling them every detail of your adult world, but it *does* mean being real with them. If you're worried about their grades, for instance, it's more effective to share that concern calmly than to come down hard with criticism.

It also means owning your mistakes. Saying something as simple as, *"I was wrong, and I'm sorry,"* can go a long way in showing them that honesty is all about authenticity. Let them know what your expectations are and why. When rules and consequences are clear from the beginning, there's less room for misunderstandings.

Teens may not always *like* the boundaries, but when they see fairness and transparency behind them, they're more likely to trust your leadership.

Reliability

Trust is built in those everyday moments—being where you said you'd be, following through on promises, and being emotionally present. If you told your teen you'd be at their soccer game, be there. If you said you'd talk later, follow through. These may seem like small things, but to your teen, they speak volumes.

Being consistent with rules is another form of reliability. If curfew changes daily or consequences vary based on your mood, it creates confusion and erodes trust. But when your teen knows what to expect—and sees that you stick to your word—they begin to understand that your guidance is steady and dependable.

Respect for Privacy

As your teen grows, their need for privacy grows too. And while that might feel scary at times, respecting their space is one of the clearest ways to say, "I trust you." That said, respecting privacy doesn't mean turning a blind eye when you sense something's off. If you're concerned—whether it's about a sudden mood change, new friends, or risky behavior—have an open, honest conversation.

Instead of snooping, say, *"Hey, I've noticed you seem withdrawn lately. I'm not here to invade your space, but I care deeply about what's going on. Can we talk about it?"* That kind of approach preserves dignity while keeping the door to connection open.

How to Respect Privacy While Staying Involved

- **Knock Before Entering**

A simple knock signals respect for their personal space. It shows that their room isn't just a place in the house—it's *their* space, and you honor that.

- **Refrain from Intrusive Actions**

Reading journals or checking phones without consent chips away at the trust you're working so hard to build. If you're tempted, pause and ask yourself: *Is this about curiosity or concern?* If it's concern, have a direct conversation instead.

- **Encourage Independence**

Let them make decisions, even the small ones. Buying their clothes, managing their schedule, or planning outings teaches responsibility. These choices build confidence, which feeds back into trust.

- **Talk About Safety with Openness**

When you're genuinely worried, don't hide it. Share your feelings with honesty: *"I trust you, but I'm worried about some things I'm noticing. Can we talk about it together?"* Teens may not open up right away, but your steady presence makes it easier for them to come to you when they're ready.

- **Set Boundaries Together**

Boundaries work best when they're created *with* your teen, not just imposed. Sit down and talk about curfews, online rules, or social media use. When your teen feels involved in the process, they're more likely to respect the rules.

- **Model Responsible Decision-Making**

Your stories matter. Share what helped you make good choices, or what happened when you didn't. Show them that mistakes are part of life, and it's how we learn and grow that really counts.

Trust isn't just built during the big conversations—it grows every day as you remain consistent, respectful, and honest. It's reinforced every time you listen without judgment, hold a boundary with love, or step back and let them try (and maybe fail) on their own.

READY FOR TAKEOFF

Equipping Teens for the Real World

"For the longest, I was slightly naive when it came to the real world. There were a lot of fears I was afraid to conquer that were just holding me back from standing up for myself or taking chances."
— Christina Milian

There comes a point when you look at your teen and think, *They're getting closer.* Closer to leaving the nest, to real-life responsibilities, and maybe, if you're honest, closer to a world that isn't always kind or predictable.

That moment comes with some form of pride and panic: Have I prepared them enough? Do they know how to speak up for themselves? Will they know how to handle setbacks, or bills, or tough conversations?

Christina Milian's quote above captures this perfectly. Many young people head out into the world a little wide-eyed, hopeful, yes, but also unsure. They might hesitate to speak up, afraid to make mistakes, or hold back from opportunities simply because they don't feel ready. But that's where we come in.

Helping our teens prepare for adulthood isn't about handing them a checklist of "how to be grown." It's about giving them the space and support to *become*. It's helping them practice decision-making while the stakes are still manageable. It's encouraging them to take chances, fall a bit, and get back up with stronger legs.

In this chapter, we're talking about the *real-world stuff*. Not just resumes or laundry (though yes, that too), but the internal skills—confidence, responsibility, resilience, assertiveness—that shape how they'll move through life. We'll talk about how to build those qualities without overwhelming them, how to create opportunities for growth right at home, and how to gently let go while still being their safety net.

It's okay if they're a little naïve at first. That's part of it. What matters most is that they leave with a sense of self-worth, the courage to take risks, and the knowledge that they are *capable*.

So, let's get started:

Nurturing Independence for the Real World

Financial Literacy

Remember the thrill of your first paycheck? It marked a step into independence, accompanied by newfound responsibilities. Financial literacy is a vital life skill that empowers teens for the real world.

- Mastering the Basics: Introduce teens to earning, spending, saving, and investing. Discuss budgeting, distinguishing needs from wants, and making informed spending choices. Familiarize them with various payment methods, from cash to digital wallets. Explain concepts like interest, loans, and the significance of emergency savings.

- Hands-On Experience: Make financial literacy practical. Involve teens in family budget planning or grocery shopping. Facilitate opening a bank account, encouraging them to save part of their allowance or job earnings. The goal is to integrate financial knowledge into daily life, building confidence for a secure financial future.

Basic Cooking Skills

- Starting Simple: Initiate with easy recipes like sandwiches or scrambled eggs. Progress to more complex dishes. Teach nutrition principles, reading food labels, and the importance of a balanced diet. Encourage exploration of various cuisines, flavor experimentation, and even recipe creation.

- Family Culinary Adventures: Transform cooking into a family affair. Initiate challenges like "cook with what you have" or designate a "make your own dinner" night. The objective isn't culinary expertise but instilling skills for preparing simple, nutritious meals independently.

Career Guidance

Career Interest Inventories

Navigational Tools

Think of career interest inventories as a guide, not something final. They're tools to help your teen reflect on what they enjoy, where their strengths lie, and how they might align with different fields.

These online assessments often ask questions like, *Do you prefer working alone or with others? Do you enjoy solving problems, helping people, and building things?* Based on their answers, the inventory suggests a list of potential career matches.

It's important to remind your teen: these results aren't set in stone. They're just opening the door to options they might not have considered.

Job Shadowing Opportunities

A Day in Their Shoes

Help your teen discover job shadowing chances in their areas of interest, whether with a veterinarian, software engineer, journalist, or chef.

Encourage them to ask questions, take notes, and reflect on the experience. *Did they find joy in the tasks?*

Did the work environment resonate with them? Could they envision themselves in a similar role?

Job shadowing provides firsthand insights into the daily facets of a career, allowing teens to comprehend the specifics and assess alignment with their interests, skills, and aspirations.

College and Career Fairs

Strategic Engagement

College and career fairs might seem like just another event on the school calendar, but they're actually golden opportunities for teens to explore what's out there and start shaping their future with confidence.

To help your teen get the most out of these events, encourage a little prep beforehand. They can look up which schools, training programs, or companies will be there and do some quick research on the ones that catch their eye. This helps them show up with purpose—and some great questions in their back pocket. For instance, they can ask about course details, campus culture, and internship opportunities.

Navigating the Transition to Adulthood

Gradual Release of Responsibility

- Early Guidance: In the initial phases of adolescence, parents and educators serve as active guides, similar to driving instructors. Here, you provide crucial direction, set boundaries, and offer structure to your teen.

- Empowerment Through Release: As they grow older, it's important to slowly step back and let them take the wheel. Start by including them in decision-making, things like planning family outings or weighing in on big life choices, like future studies or career paths. Let them manage their time, take on new responsibilities, and even make mistakes. These are the moments where confidence takes root.

This shift doesn't happen overnight, though; it's a gradual, thoughtful process. It's about finding that balance between supporting them and trusting them to stand on their own.

Open Dialogues on Adulthood Realities

- Transparent Conversations: Keep the lines of communication open. Talk about what adulthood really looks like, not just the freedom, but also the responsibilities that come with it. Be honest, but also reassuring. Let them know you're there as a guide, not a judge.

- Informative Discussions: Keep in mind that these conversations are not about imposing expectations but rather enlightening them on the realities of adulthood. It's a preparatory dialogue, helping them comprehend the transformations they will undergo and equipping them for the journey ahead.

Celebrating Milestones

When your teen reaches a milestone, like landing their first job (even if just part-time), graduating, or getting that college acceptance, take a moment to celebrate. These aren't just boxes to check; they're markers of growth, of determination, of all the effort they've put in along the way.

These milestone celebrations serve as acknowledgments of their growth, expressions of gratitude for their efforts, and confidence boosters as they embrace the challenges and triumphs of adulthood.

CONCLUSION

Raising a teenager isn't something you prepare for with a checklist. It's something you live through, sometimes patiently, sometimes clumsily, often with a full heart and an exhausted spirit. And yet, here you are, showing up, learning, and adapting to make sure you do the best you can. That alone speaks volumes.

Over the past chapters, we've explored the adolescent brain from the inside out. We've looked at the emotional storms, the academic hurdles, the moments of defiance, and the victories. Through it all is a single truth: *your presence matters more than perceived perfection.*

Understanding how your teen's mind is changing helps you respond with more clarity and less frustration. Recognizing their emotional needs builds the kind of trust that outlasts tantrums and tempers. And supporting their academic journey—not with pressure, but with encouragement—can help them fall in love with learning, not just achievement.

I say this not as an expert in a white coat, but as a mother who's walked this path with two sons. I've seen firsthand how easy it is to feel overwhelmed, to question if you're doing enough–or too much. There were days when I felt like I was losing them to mood swings or silence. But slowly, through listening without fixing, guiding without forcing, and loving without condition, we became a team.

If there's one thing I've learned, it's this: teenagers don't need perfect parents. They need present ones. They need people willing to learn beside them, cry with them, laugh with them, and sometimes, just sit in the same room without saying a word.

So let this be your gentle reminder: every rough patch is an opportunity for growth. Every argument holds the potential for reconnection. And every time you choose to stay soft, even when everything feels hard, you are building the foundation to a solid relationship with your teen.

As we close this book, I leave you with this:

Be the lighthouse, not the lifeboat. You don't need to rescue them from every storm, but you do need to shine, steady and sure, so they always know how to find their way home.

Offer them roots, so they feel safe. Wings, so they feel free. And love, so they never doubt their worth.

Let them make mistakes. Let them fall and then be there when they rise. That rising, however slow, however messy, is what this whole journey is about.

With all my heart,

From one parent to another—

You've got this.

BOOK THOUGHTS & OPINIONS

Dear Readers,

I am writing to express my deepest gratitude for your support in reading my book. Your time and engagement mean the world to me. If you've enjoyed the journey through these pages, please consider leaving a review. Your words can guide and inspire other parents and educators, helping them discover the book and decide if it's the right fit for them.

Reviews are the lifeblood of independent authors, and your honest feedback can make a significant impact. Thank you for being a part of my literary journey, and I look forward to hearing from you.

To leave a review, go to your Order History, find the book under your purchases, and click "Write a Product Review." If you're in the US, you can also scan the QR code below for quick access.

With gratitude,

Joyce T.

🎁 BONUS GIFT

As a gesture of gratitude, I'm delighted to offer you a complimentary copy of the e-book Bundled 2-in-1, aimed at enhancing your understanding of your child. This resource provides a comprehensive exploration of child development, spanning from embryo to teen.

Adolescent Brain 101 + Simplifying Child Development 2-in-1 Bundle

A Stage-by-Stage Guide to Nurturing a Healthy Child's Mind from Embryo to Teen

Scan the QR code to download with Access Code: mind

www.JoyceTbooks.com

REFERENCES

American Psychological Association. (n.d.). The adolescent brain: Beyond raging hormones. Harvard Health Publishing. Retrieved from https://www.health.harvard.edu/mind-and-mood/the-adolescent-brain-beyond-raging-hormones

Bureau of Labor Statistics. (2015). Career planning for high schoolers. Retrieved from https://www.bls.gov/careeroutlook/2015/article/pdf/career-planning-for-high-schoolers.pdf

Center for Parenting Education. (n.d.). The skill of listening. Retrieved from https://centerforparentingeducation.org/library-of-articles/healthy-communication/the-skill-of-listening/

Cho, S., & Hall, J. R. (2016). Pubertal development, emotion regulatory styles, and the... National Center for Biotechnology Information. Retrieved from https://www.ncbi.nlm.nih.gov/pmc/articles/PMC

5061504/#:~:text=In%20this%20sense%2C%20
adolescents%20with,diminish%20emotional%20
clarity%20over%20time.

Choosing Therapy. (n.d.). Does my teen need
counseling? 15 signs to know. Retrieved from
https://www.choosingtherapy.com/does-my-teen-
need-counseling/

Daniel Wong. (2022, June 14). How to
communicate with teenagers (11 actionable tips).
Retrieved from https://www.daniel-
wong.com/2022/06/14/communicating-with-
teens/

Empowering Parents. (n.d.). Hope for parents of
defiant teens: 6 ways to parent more effectively.
Retrieved from
https://www.empoweringparents.com/article/hop
e-for-parents-of-defiant-teens-6-ways-to-parent-
more-effectively/

Focus on the Family. (n.d.). Independence or
rebellion? Retrieved from
https://www.focusonthefamily.com/parenting/ind
ependence-or-rebellion/

Good Therapy. (n.d.). Punishments vs.
consequences: Teach your teen the difference.
Retrieved from
https://www.goodtherapy.org/blog/punishments-
vs-consequences-teach-your-teen-the-difference-
0427155/

Gottman Institute. (n.d.). Building trust with
teenagers. Retrieved from
https://www.gottman.com/blog/building-trust-
with-teenagers/

Greater Good Science Center. (n.d.). How the teen
brain transforms relationships. Retrieved from
https://greatergood.berkeley.edu/article/item/how
_the_teen_brain_transforms_relationships

Harvard Health Publishing. (n.d.). The adolescent
brain: Beyond raging hormones. Harvard Health
Publishing. Retrieved from
https://www.health.harvard.edu/mind-and-
mood/the-adolescent-brain-beyond-raging-
hormones

Harvard Medical School. (n.d.). Screen time and the
brain. Retrieved from
https://hms.harvard.edu/news/screen-time-brain

Lessonbee. (n.d.). How social media can affect teenage self-esteem. Retrieved from https://lessonbee.com/blog/how-social-media-can-affect-teenage-self-esteem

LinkedIn. (n.d.). Digital detox and mental well-being: Examining the benefits... Retrieved from https://www.linkedin.com/pulse/digital-detox-mental-well-being-examining-benefits-unplugging-teenagers?trk=news-guest_share-article#:~:text=In%20conclusion%2C%20a%20digital%20detox,and%20promote%20healthier%20sleep%20patterns.

Mayo Clinic. (n.d.). Teen depression - Symptoms and causes. Retrieved from https://www.mayoclinic.org/diseases-conditions/teen-depression/symptoms-causes/syc-20350985

Michigan Department of Education. (2013, June 21). Adolescents: Discipline with the brain in mind. Retrieved from https://www.michigan.gov/-/media/Project/Websites/mde/2013/11/01/Tips_for_Effective_Discipline_6-21-

13.pdf?rev=50e829e1b22542989396606c0a017c1
1f

Middle Earth. (2014, April 14). 5 ways parents can
teach assertiveness to teens. Retrieved from
https://middleearthnj.org/2014/04/14/5-ways-
parents-can-teach-assertiveness-to-teens/

National Academies. (n.d.). Open Case Studies:
Mental Health of American Youth. Retrieved
from https://www.opencasestudies.org/ocs-bp-
youth-mental-health/

National Center for Biotechnology Information.
(n.d.). Adolescent risk-taking, impulsivity, and
brain development. Retrieved from
https://www.ncbi.nlm.nih.gov/pmc/articles/PMC
3445337/

National Center for Biotechnology Information.
(n.d.). Later school start time: The impact of sleep
on academic... Retrieved from
https://www.ncbi.nlm.nih.gov/pmc/articles/PMC
7177233/

National Center for Biotechnology Information.
(n.d.). Prevalence and risk factors of cyberbullying
and its... Retrieved from

https://www.ncbi.nlm.nih.gov/pmc/articles/PMC
9860135/

National Center for Biotechnology Information.
(n.d.). Stress and the developing adolescent brain
- PMC. Retrieved from
https://www.ncbi.nlm.nih.gov/pmc/articles/PMC
3601560/

National Center for Biotechnology Information.
(n.d.). The emerging neuroscience of intrinsic
motivation - PMC. Retrieved from
https://www.ncbi.nlm.nih.gov/pmc/articles/PMC
5364176/

National Center for Biotechnology Information.
(n.d.). The influence of academic pressure on
adolescents... Retrieved from
https://www.ncbi.nlm.nih.gov/pmc/articles/PMC
9534181/

National Center for Biotechnology Information.
(n.d.). Types of parenting styles and effects on
children. Retrieved from
https://www.ncbi.nlm.nih.gov/books/NBK56874
3/

National University. (2022, January 20). Mindset and academic success: What's the connection? Retrieved from https://www.national.edu/2022/01/20/how-mindset-can-help-academic-success/

Parent & Teen. (n.d.). Building resilience in teens: The 7 Cs. Retrieved from https://parentandteen.com/building-resilience-in-teens/

Positive Psychology. (n.d.). 16 delayed gratification exercises, worksheets & activities. Retrieved from https://positivepsychology.com/delayed-gratification-exercises-worksheets/

Positive Psychology. (n.d.). Promoting self-regulation in adolescents and young adults. Retrieved from https://fpg.unc.edu/sites/fpg.unc.edu/files/resources/reports-and-policy-briefs/Promoting%20Self-Regulation%20in%20Adolescents%20and%20Young%20Adults.pdf

RBC Wealth Management. (n.d.). Why financial literacy is an important life skill for youths. Retrieved from https://www.rbcwealthmanagement.com/enca/insights/why-financial-literacy-is-an-important-life-skill-for-youths

SheKnows. (n.d.). 24 essential cooking & baking skills your teen should... Retrieved from https://www.sheknows.com/food-and-recipes/articles/1140231/cooking-skills-for-teens/

UNC Frank Porter Graham Child Development Institute. (n.d.). Effects of mindfulness-based intervention on adolescents. Retrieved from https://www.ncbi.nlm.nih.gov/pmc/articles/PMC8701759/

UNC Frank Porter Graham Child Development Institute. (n.d.). Promoting self-regulation in adolescents and young adults. Retrieved from https://fpg.unc.edu/sites/fpg.unc.edu/files/resources/reports-and-policy-briefs/Promoting%20Self-Regulation%20in%20Adolescents%20and%20Young%20Adults.pdf

UNICEF Innocenti Research Centre. (n.d.). The Adolescent Brain: A second window of opportunity. Retrieved from https://www.unicef-irc.org/publications/pdf/adolescent_brain_a_second_window_of_opportunity_a_compendium.pdf

University of Nebraska-Lincoln Extension. (n.d.).
Friendships, peer influence, and peer pressure
during... Retrieved from
https://extensionpublications.unl.edu/assets/html/
g1751/build/g1751.htm

Verywell Family. (n.d.). 8 essential strategies for
raising a confident teen. Retrieved from
https://www.verywellfamily.com/essential-
strategies-for-raising-a-confident-teen-2611002